EARLY YEARS
ACTIVITY CHEST

Supply teaching

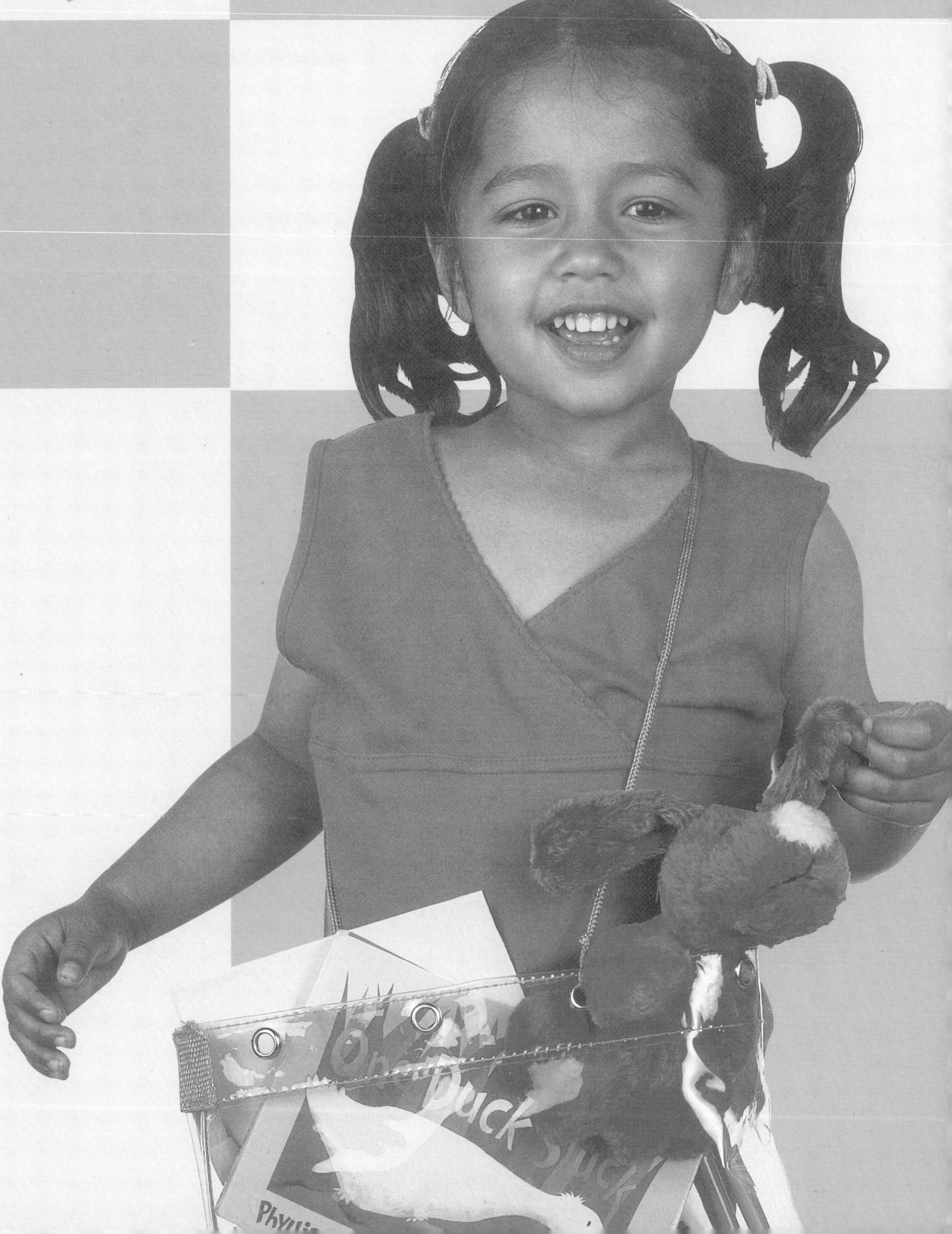

British Library Cataloguing-in-Publication Data
A catalogue record for this book is available from the British Library.

ISBN 0 439 98313 4

The right of Irene Yates to be identified as the author of this work has been asserted by her in accordance with the Copyright, Designs and Patents Act 1988.

AUTHOR
Irene Yates

EDITOR
Lesley Sudlow

ASSISTANT EDITOR
Saveria Mezzana

SERIES DESIGNER
Lynne Joesbury

DESIGNER
Paul Cheshire

ILLUSTRATIONS
Pete Smith

COVER PHOTOGRAPH
Martyn Chillmaid

Text © 2002 Irene Yates
© 2002 Scholastic Ltd
Designed using Adobe Pagemaker
Published by Scholastic Ltd, Villiers House,
Clarendon Avenue, Leamington Spa, Warwickshire CV32 5PR
Printed by Alden Group Ltd, Oxford
Visit our website at www.scholastic.co.uk

1 2 3 4 5 6 7 8 9 0   2 3 4 5 6 7 8 9 0 1

CONTENTS

CONTENTS

Introduction

It is an enormous responsibility to be 'on supply' with very young children. The children may feel very insecure when their known helper is away for whatever reason, and possibly be shy because someone new, whom they do not know, is coming to take their place. They might feel confused because they do not know whether to expect the routine that they are familiar with, or whether it will be different. They may even feel a little afraid, because something – and someone – new and unknown can be very daunting.

Your priority, therefore, has always got to be to lead the children into feeling safe, secure, comfortable and happy. You need to achieve this at the same time that you are:

- trying to get to know the children as a group and as individuals
- checking out the resources and trying to locate everything
- establishing the levels at which the children are moving towards the Early Learning Goals
- working out which stage of development each child has reached
- deciding which of the children's daily routines you need to stick to rigidly in order not to make the day harder for them and for you
- trying to form links with the children's parents or carers and find out a little about their backgrounds.

The aim of this book

The activities in this book will enable you to carry out your role as well as giving the children opportunities to work towards solid goals across all six Areas of Learning. The book is closely linked to the Early Learning Goals (Qualifications and Curriculum Authority) and contains six chapters, one for each of the Areas:

- Personal, social and emotional development
- Communication, language and literacy
- Mathematical development
- Knowledge and understanding of the world
- Physical development
- Creative development.

The ideas are equally applicable to the documents on pre-school education published for Scotland, Wales and Northern Ireland.

How to use this book

At the beginning of each activity, you will find a key learning objective which outlines the specific skills, concepts or attitudes that the activity is designed to focus upon. However, since all Areas of Learning are interdependent, every task provides the children with opportunities for development across the curriculum and aims to support and build upon their self-confidence and self-esteem, as well as their awareness of others and respect for one another's contributions.

Many of the activities contain opportunities for negotiation while they are happening and for discussion after the tasks are completed. This is particularly so for the art and craft activities in Chapter 6, when the children are combining their knowledge, experience and ideas to bring about something different. Talking together about choosing materials and deciding where to put them and how they should be fixed can ensure that the children's expectations broaden – they begin to be aware that there is not always a 'right' way but that their interaction can bring about a 'new' way.

Reluctant children can be helped to acquire a measure of self-confidence by becoming part of the small team that negotiates in a safe but flexible environment. The discussion of how successful the task was, at the end of the activity, is crucial to the nature of the shared experience – everyone is encouraged to arrange their thoughts and ideas into talk. This experience can give the children a sense of their own value, presenting them with the opportunity to express ideas and opinions or defend decisions which, in turn, will enrich the quality of their experiences.

The activities

The activities in this book are designed to be short, stand-alone time-fillers. Most of them will take between ten and 20 minutes, although some of them can be extended to 30 minutes.

Each activity is presented on a single page. It gives a key learning objective, a suggested size of group and a list of the resources that you will need to carry it out. The group size is only a recommendation, but will give you an idea of how many children it is possible to work with at a time, and, of course, you may need to adapt to the size of group that you find yourself working with. Obviously, much depends upon the ratio of adult to child and upon the resources that are available to you.

When needed, there is a 'Preparation' section on how to get ready for the activity before you introduce it to the children. The activities are then explained, step by step, in the 'What to do' section, and suggestions are made for supporting the children where necessary, and for extending their learning when possible. Indeed, although each activity is designed to be used with an 'average' four-year old, the children will all be at different stages of development. So this book offers 'Support' ideas aimed at children who are younger or at earlier stages, and 'Extension' ideas for children who are older or who may be able to accomplish the tasks in a shorter period of time.

Using the photocopiable sheets

There are 12 photocopiable sheets at the end of the book, which support some of the activities. Information is given in the relevant activity on how many sheets you will need to prepare, for example, one per child or one per small group. Sticking or copying the photocopiable sheets on to card, then laminating them, will help to keep them in good condition. The photocopiable sheets are task-orientated in order to give the children an opportunity to reinforce their acquisition of the skills, concepts and attitudes that the activity provides.

Using resources

Someone working as a 'supply' cannot be sure what resources they will find in any one setting – some groups have everything you could wish for, while some groups have next to nothing. This book focuses on the perspective of having next to nothing. You should not assume that you will walk into every setting and find a complete set of Lego, six tricycles or a state-of-the-art computer, but it is fairly likely that at some point you will be able to obtain corrugated card, cardboard boxes, parcel tape and other similar items.

Many of the activities do not require any resources other than the enthusiasm of the children, yourself and perhaps their parents or carers. It is possible to adapt and to improvise. Easily available materials, the natural world and the children's own environment can provide as good a model and stimulus for learning and developing as any commercial 'must-have' equipment!

Being involved in supply, you will find more than ever that learning begins with the learner. If you start from their own points, the children's natural curiosity and interest will often take over and inspire you to even greater ideas.

Links with home

Each activity has a section entitled 'Home links', which suggests ways to draw carers into extending and supporting the experiences that their children have been sharing. The term 'carer' has been used to suggest parents, foster parents, family members, friends or others who may look after the children when they return home.

Multicultural links

Where possible, ideas have been suggested to adapt or extend the activities so that the children can learn more about other cultures and other parts of the world, while they are carrying out their tasks or after they have completed them.

You may not always be familiar with the religious and cultural traditions of the community served by the setting. In this situation, the children's families will be able to provide essential links with the local community. The onus will be on you to extend your own knowledge as quickly as possible, in a sensitive way, by interacting with the carers. This interaction with, and involvement of, the carers and community leaders can help to create a most rewarding and enriching supportive environment.

CHAPTER 1

Personal, social and emotional development

The activities in this chapter will help you to become familiar with the children and to develop their ability to work as part of a group and be aware of themselves and others. Ideas include talking about feelings, understanding a secret rule and taking turns while playing games.

GROUP SIZE
Up to six children.

TIMING
30 minutes.

HOME LINKS
Suggest to carers that they tell their children about any unusual parties that they have been to, when they were either young or grown up, such as wedding parties, street parties or parties to celebrate special events.

MULTICULTURAL LINKS
Be aware of festival days from other cultures. Plan your party around specific festivals and decorate headbands in appropriate styles.

LET'S PARTY!

Learning objective
To be confident to try new activities and initiate ideas.

What you need
Coloured card or sugar paper; sticky tape; scissors; stapler; coloured paper; sticky shapes; crayons; felt-tipped pens; scraps of fabric.

Preparation
Cut the card or sugar paper into strips (20cm high) to fit around the children's heads.

What to do
Talk with the children about parties. Invite them to tell you and the rest of the group what kind of parties they have been to and what happens at parties. Ask specific questions such as, 'Whose party was it?', 'What did you like about the party?'.

Tell the children that you can have a party for any reason, or on any theme that you wish. Think of ideas for a new kind of party and write them down as a list. Suggest some ideas of your own to encourage the children to contribute, for example, a garden party, happy day party, let's-be-friends party, magic animals' party, rainy-day party and so on.

Discuss headwear that the children could wear. For example, if they have chosen a garden-party theme, they could make their headbands look like flower gardens, or they could draw smiley faces for a happy-day party. Encourage the children to contribute their own ideas and to decorate the headbands how they wish, using the resources available. Staple or tape the headbands together to fit individual children.

Support
Help the children to verbalize their ideas with confidence and encourage them to listen attentively and develop ideas.

Extension
If time allows, hold the party with the whole group. Arrange biscuits, drinks and appropriate games. Use the book *Where the Wild Things Are* by Maurice Sendak (Red Fox) for ideas for a 'wild rumpus'. Sort out some rules for the 'wild rumpus' when the children start playing.

GROUP SIZE
Up to eight children.

TIME
15 minutes.

HOW ARE YOU TODAY?

Learning objective
To develop awareness of the feelings of others.

What you need
Large pieces of card; board; marker pen.

What to do
Sit with the children in a comfortable space. Tell them that you are feeling very happy today because you have come to be with them. Ask, 'Is anyone else feeling happy?'. Then ask individuals, 'Why are you feeling happy today?'. Discuss the children's replies.

On one piece of card, write the word 'happy', pointing out the direction in which you write and sounding out the beginning of the word. Choose a child who feels happy and say, 'Charlotte feels *happy*', showing the word as you say it.

Then ask, 'Who does not feel happy today?'. When someone replies, ask how he or she feels. Do they know a word for their feeling? What is making them feel like this? Alternatively, ask, 'Who feels *sad* today?' and, again, explore the feeling of being sad. Ask, 'How should we behave towards someone who feels sad?'.

Go through the process of finding words in order to develop the children's vocabulary for different feelings, for example, sad, cross, unwell, miserable, excited, proud, eager and so on. Write the words on the board, demonstrating how you write and saying each word aloud as you write it.

Support
Help the children to empathize with one another by explaining that we all have these feelings at different times and that is how we know how to behave towards one another.

Extension
Make a display of the words and use them in a word-recognition task. Look in books for characters that display specific feelings such as *What Makes Me Happy* by Catherine and Laurence Anholt (Walker Books).

HOME LINKS
Invite the children to paint or draw 'feeling' pictures showing themselves or someone else being happy, sad, excited or disappointed. Scribe for them, or help them to write emergently a caption for their pictures. Let them take the pictures home to share and talk about with their carers.

MULTICULTURAL LINKS
Look for story-books that show children in other countries and from other traditions, in situations where their faces are expressing emotions.

GROUP SIZE
Up to 15 children.

TIMING
15 to 20 minutes.

WHISPERING WOLVES

Learning objective
To maintain attention and concentration.

What you need
A large, open space.

Preparation
Practise quiet and loud whispers with the children.

What to do
Explain to the children that you are going to play a game called 'Whispering wolves' and that they will need to listen carefully and concentrate very hard so that they know what to do. The child who is the 'Whispering Wolf' should face the other children and think of an action to challenge them. The wolf then says, in a loud whisper, 'I am the Whispering Wolf and I am going to gobble you up, but not if you can...'. The wolf then gives an instruction, in a loud whisper, for example, 'stand on one leg while I count to five', 'do ten jumps', 'put your hands on your knees' and so on.

Demonstrate the actions of the Whispering Wolf to the children, speaking in a loud whisper so that they understand the level of volume needed. Do two or three quick-fire actions and then let the children play the game. Ask who would like to be the wolf first. Make sure that the child who is volunteering has a good idea for a first action and whispers it loud enough for the others to hear.

Encourage the children to do the actions, then ask them to quickly and quietly sit down. The Whispering Wolf should then choose another child to be the wolf.

Try to ensure that each child has a chance to be the Whispering Wolf. Each wolf should try to think of a different action. Be ready with lots of action ideas in case the children cannot think of any, such as 'turn around three times', 'jump up and sit down twice', 'take ten fairy footsteps forwards', 'take three long steps backwards', 'curl up in a ball, count to five then stand up' and so on. Make it a 'quick-fire' game so that the children do not get bored and lose concentration.

Support
Be aware of any children with a hearing impairment and show them the actions. Help any children with physical impairment to get as close to the actions as they can.

Extension
Take on the role of the Whispering Wolf. Name an individual child and give instructions that you know are appropriate to them.

HOME LINKS
Suggest to carers that they play games such as 'Simon says' and 'Statues' with their children at home to develop their attention and concentration.

GROUP SIZE
Up to 15 children.

TIMING
15 to 20 minutes.

MY NAME IS...

Learning objective
To form good relationships with adults.

What you need
Paper or card; board; marker pen; Blu-Tack.

Preparation
Cut the paper or card into pieces (approximately 15cm x 6cm).

What to do
Explain to the children that you want to learn all of their names, and them to learn your name. Tell them that you would like each child to give you their name and to say something that they like doing. Demonstrate to them by saying, 'My name is Maria and I like coming to be with you when (name of usual helper) is not here'. Write your name clearly on a piece of paper or card, show it to the children, pointing from left to right, and read it out.

Encourage the children to respond in the same way, for example, 'My name is Sanjay and I like playing in the sand'. Write the child's name clearly on another piece of paper or card, sounding it out where appropriate, discussing what sound it begins with and so on, and reading it back to the children. If there are any children with the same names, write them in a different colour or add a second name so that you can differentiate them. When you have written out all the name cards, attach them to the board with Blu-Tack. Learn the children's names by calling each child and asking them to come to find their name card on the board.

Support
If necessary, help the children to speak confidently.

Extension
Invite the children to sit in a circle and when they introduce themselves, ask them to also introduce the person sitting on their left, for example, 'My name is Ishpal and this is James.'

HOME LINKS
Invite the children to take home a picture of something that they have done that day, with your name on as well as theirs, so that their carers know who you are.

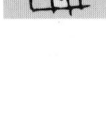

MULTICULTURAL LINKS
Write 'What is your name?' in different languages on separate pieces of card or paper and make a wall display with them.

GROUP SIZE
Up to eight children.

TIMING
Ten minutes.

TAKING TURNS

Learning objective
To work as part of a group, taking turns.

What you need
No special equipment.

What to do
Sit in a circle with the children. Talk about the things that they can do. Begin the discussion by asking, 'Who can jump?', 'Who can hop?', 'Who can draw with a pencil?' and so on. When the children have remembered lots of examples of things that they can do, play a game. The person who is 'on' should say their name and perform an action without saying what it is. They must not perform an action that someone else has carried out. Once the children understand the rules, encourage them to role-play actions such as driving a car, ironing clothes, cleaning the windows, shopping and so on.

The first person to be 'on' should go into the centre of the circle and say, 'I am (name) and I can do this (dramatizes action)'. The rest of the children should put up their hands to be chosen to verbalize the action. If the first child you choose is correct, they must go into the centre and perform another action.

As you go around the circle inviting children to have a turn, verbalize all the time, for example, 'Now, it must be Joe's turn', 'Oh, Lisa, you just had a turn, didn't you?', 'Manish, how many turns have you had?' and so on, so that the children become aware of the procedure of turn-taking. Try to make sure that everyone has the same number of turns.

Support
Help the children as necessary to think of new actions, rather than copy or repeat ones that have already been done.

Extension
Play the game with the children going around the circle in order. Encourage the child on the left of the one who is 'on' to verbalize the actions, then let them have a turn.

HOME LINKS
Tell carers that you have been taking turns and encourage them to play with their children at home games that require turn-taking, for example, *Snakes and Ladders*.

LET'S BE FRIENDS

Learning objective
To understand what is right, what is wrong, and why.

What you need
The photocopiable sheet on page 69; pencils; board; marker pen.

Preparation
Make an enlarged copy of the photocopiable sheet and enough A4 copies for each pair of children to share for the discussion, and one for each child to complete at the end of the session.

What to do
Sit the children in pairs and give one copy of the photocopiable sheet to each pair. Display the enlarged copy on the board. Look at the pictures with the children and explain that they tell a story such as in a comic. Focus on the first frame. Ask, 'Where do you think the bears are?' and 'What are they doing?'. Encourage the children to verbalize as much as possible.

Focus on the second frame. Ask, 'What's happening in this picture?' and 'Why do you think the bear is alone?'. Help the children to find the correct words to describe how she looks, for example, sad, unhappy, lonely, upset, left out and so on. Encourage the children to express the bear's feelings in their own words, but if necessary offer more vocabulary to help them.

Show the children the third picture and ask them what they think is happening. Repeat with the fourth picture. Talk about the implications of the bear being left out. At this point in the discussion, the children will probably identify with the lonely bear, but they need to think about the feelings and actions of the other bears. Invite them to describe them, for example, spiteful, mean, unkind, unfriendly, cruel and so on. Ask them why they think that the bears are acting this way. Do they think it is good to act like this? What would be a much nicer way to act?

Give out further copies of the photocopiable sheet so that each child has one. Invite them to complete the last frame so that the story has a happy ending.

Support
Be aware of any vulnerable children who might be victims of this kind of behaviour, and look for ways to make them feel comfortable.

Extension
Talk about what it feels like to be left out and ask the children to tell you about any time when it happened to them or when they have done it to someone else. Do they know why they did it?

BUSY BEETLES

Learning objective
To work as part of a group, sharing fairly.

What you need
The photocopiable sheet on page 70; 1–6 dice; pencils.

Preparation
Show the children how to throw a dice and how to 'read' it. Make a copy of the photocopiable sheet for each child and one for discussion.

What to do
Examine the photocopiable sheet with the children. Show them the busy beetle scurrying along at the top of the page. Then look at the four pictures of just a head and a body and explain that these four beetles cannot scurry along until they have the rest of their bodies drawn in. Each busy beetle needs two antennae, two eyes, six legs, two wings and one pointy tail.

Explain to the children that they should take turns to throw the dice, work out which part of the body corresponds with the number that is shown on the dice, then draw it on the blank body.

Give each child a pencil and a copy of the photocopiable sheet. Invite the children to take turns to throw the dice, drawing in the appropriate body part to the corresponding number. However, if, for example, they throw a 2 and both of the eyes are drawn in, they have to wait for their next throw before they can draw anything.

Encourage the children to develop the attitude of working together as a team to draw the busy beetle, not to compete with one another.

Support
Help the children to interpret the numbers or count the spots on the dice if necessary. Remind them occasionally which number relates to which body part.

Extension
When all the children have played the game several times, help them to cut out the completed busy beetles and make a display of them scurrying across a wall.

'AND STOP!'

Learning objective
To understand that there needs to be agreed values and codes of behaviour.

What you need
No special equipment.

What to do
Explain to the children that there are lots of times during the session when you will need them to stop what they are doing, be very quiet and listen to you. Discuss when and why this might be, for example, when something goes wrong, when it is almost time for a drink, when everything needs to be tidied away or when you need to talk to the children all together.

To help you and the children, you need to have a little rule so that everyone knows when to stop. Tell the children that your own secret rule is that you like to whisper 'And stop!'. Explain to the group that when you say these words, you would like everyone to put down what they are doing straight away, stop talking and move to a special place, for example, at the tables or on the mat. Make sure that your choice is clear to all the children. To make it easier for them to follow the rule, focus on their hands or arms and ask them to put their hands on their heads or to fold their arms.

Next, practise your rule. Say to the children, 'Pretend to carry on with what you are doing, but listen out for me whispering "And stop!"'. Invite them to go back to their activities and when you see that they are all busy, whisper 'And stop!'. As they will be waiting the first time, you will probably get an excellent response, so give plenty of positive encouragement.

Repeat this exercise several times throughout the session, until the children understand the procedure. At the end of the session, talk again with them about why it is necessary to have a rule like this. Carry it on throughout your stay with the class or group, until it becomes second nature to them.

Support
If necessary, explain the rules to the children individually.

Extension
Use non-verbal instructions to communicate with the children. For example, tell them that if you put your arms in the air it means that you want them to listen, if you fold your arms that you want them to talk quietly, and so on.

GROUP SIZE
Up to eight children.

TIMING
20 minutes.

I CAN DO IT

Learning objective
To use resources independently.

What you need
Tables; paints; crayons; felt-tipped pens; felt pieces; glue; stickers; scrap fabric pieces; buttons; wool; recyclable materials; scissors; sticky shapes; large sheets of paper.

Preparation
Decide on a theme, perhaps to link with topic work, for example, cats.

What to do
Explain to the children that you would like them to portray a cat. Think of all the different ways that they might do this and list them. For example, they could draw it, paint it, cut and stick it, make a junk model, make a collage and so on. Encourage as many ideas as possible and spend some time exploring all the possibilities. Ask questions such as, 'How would you do that?' and 'What would you need for that?' so that the children understand what materials they would need.

Set up some tables ready for the children to create their portraits. Give the children complete freedom to decide how they will portray their cats, then invite them to select their own materials without any help.

Some children may be reluctant to choose their own resources, so give them plenty of help, asking them which kinds of materials they would prefer. Encourage them to find some 'feely' fabric and draw the cat for them if necessary.

Support
Children may be more ambitious than their skills allow them to execute, so be ready to assist. The focus of the activity is on developing their ability to make selections with as little assistance as possible. If problems arise, make suggestions where necessary on how they might use what they have chosen.

Help the children to persevere to the end of their task, allowing them as much choice as you can while still guiding them.

HOME LINKS
Encourage carers to allow their children to collect their own coats, bags and so on and get themselves ready for going home.

Extension
Use all possible opportunities for the children to develop independence – for example, ask them to sort out the pencils, crayons and felt-tipped pens. Encourage them to choose activities for themselves.

GROUP SIZE
Up to ten children.

TIMING
Four sessions of ten to 15 minutes.

I FEEL HAPPY

Learning objective

To develop an awareness of their own feelings and be sensitive to the feelings of others.

What you need

The photocopiable sheet on page 71.

Preparation

Make a copy of the photocopiable sheet for each child.

What to do

Talk to the children about what makes everyone feel happy. Invite individual children to tell you what makes them happy. Ask, 'How can you tell when somebody is happy?'. Encourage the children to tell you as much as they have absorbed about body language, for example, 'When somebody is happy their eyes twinkle' and give lots of positive reinforcement.

Invite the children to sit on the floor with their heads down. Tell them to pretend that they are at home and very fed up because they do not know what to do. Suddenly, there is a knock at the door and their best friend has come to ask them to play. Can they make a happy face to show how they feel?

Give each child a copy of the photocopiable sheet and show them the four blank faces on it. Suggest that in the first space they draw themselves or someone else looking happy.

In the writing space, use demonstrated writing, emergent writing, tracing or copying techniques, depending on the children's abilities, to write either the word 'happy' or a short phrase or sentence such as 'I am happy' or 'My friend is happy'.

At the next sessions, repeat the process with 'sad', 'cross' or 'angry' and 'tired'. Tell stories that the children can imagine, such as 'You have been waiting for your birthday to come because you are sure that you are going to get the present that you really want, but when you open it, it's something different' or 'You have been looking forward to playing with your friend, but when the time comes he goes to play with someone else'.

Support

Some children may need help with 'reading' body language and expression, so carry out role-play exercises where two children act out a situation to promote a particular feeling.

Extension

Talk about the things that we do that influence other people's feelings. Ask the children for ideas about how they would make other children or adults feel happy, sad and so on.

HOME LINKS
Ask carers to encourage their children to make someone else happy at home, for example, by tidying away their toys or playing with a younger sibling.

MULTICULTURAL LINKS
Cut out pictures of people from other cultures and traditions showing emotions, and make them part of the display to show that people from all over the world have the same ways of showing that they are happy or sad.

CHAPTER 2

In this chapter you will find activities to develop the children's communication, language and literacy skills while you get to know them. The ideas include improvising role-play, retelling familiar stories and playing a memory game.

Communication, language and literacy

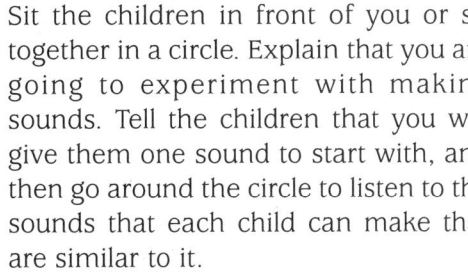

SILLY WORDS

Learning objective
To explore and experiment with sound

What you need
Board; marker pen.

What to do
Sit the children in front of you or s together in a circle. Explain that you ar going to experiment with makin sounds. Tell the children that you w give them one sound to start with, an then go around the circle to listen to th sounds that each child can make tha are similar to it.

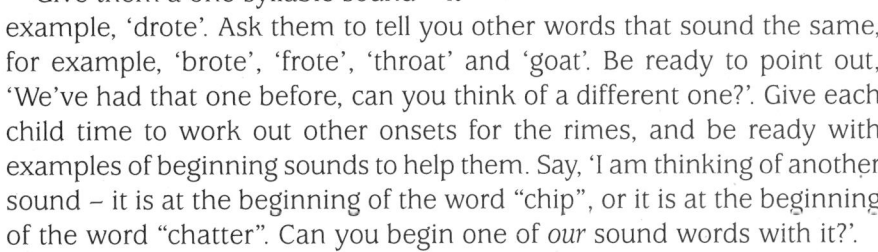

Give them a one-syllable sound – it example, 'drote'. Ask them to tell you other words that sound the same, for example, 'brote', 'frote', 'throat' and 'goat'. Be ready to point out, 'We've had that one before, can you think of a different one?'. Give each child time to work out other onsets for the rimes, and be ready with examples of beginning sounds to help them. Say, 'I am thinking of another sound – it is at the beginning of the word "chip", or it is at the beginning of the word "chatter". Can you begin one of *our* sound words with it?'.

Write some of the more interesting sounds on the board, showing the children how to write them as you are doing it. When the children suggest 'real words', stop and say, 'I think this is a real word, isn't it? What does it mean?'.

Go on to two-syllable sounds, for example, 'bliffle', and repeat the process. Have fun thinking up 'new' and 'silly' words and talk about what they might mean. When the children know how to play the game, try three-syllable sounds, for example, 'blubadrub'. Give them lots of time to think and experiment with the sounds.

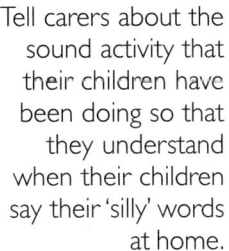

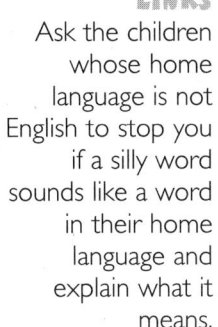

Support
Be aware of any children with hearing impairments, or children who cannot hear beginning sounds clearly, and help them to join in.

Extension
Make up a story or rhyme using the children's favourite silly sounds.

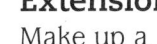

ELEPHANTS' FEET

Learning objective
To listen and respond to rhymes.

What you need
A large, open space for the children to move about safely.

Preparation
Teach the children this rhyme:
> 'Elephants' feet
> Are always neat
> When they come walking down the street!'.

What to do
Say the rhyme together. Explain to the children that you would like them to find alternative words for 'walking'. Suggest your own word, for example, 'marching', and ask the children to be the elephants, coming 'neatly down the street' in the way that you suggest, saying, 'Elephants' feet are always neat when they come marching down the street'. Encourage the children to listen for the word 'marching' and to march until you tell them to stop and sit down.

Invite a child to stand up and recite the whole rhyme, including their chosen word. They might say 'tiptoeing', 'dancing', 'hopping', 'running', 'galloping', 'jumping', 'leaping', 'skipping' and so on. Ask the rest of the children to stand up and move around in the way that the added word asks them to, while saying the rhyme. At the end of the rhyme, they should sit down and let another child have a turn. Remind the children to keep the elephants' feet 'neat' while they are moving, to stop them crashing into one another!

Support
Give plenty of encouragement and assistance to the children who find it difficult to stand in front of the others and say the rhyme. Suggest words for them if they are unable to think of one.

Extension
Invite the children to paint pictures of elephants coming down the street in specific ways and display them with the words of the rhyme at the top. Write the word that describes how the elephant is coming down the street next to each picture. Use the display as a shared reading experience.

GROUP SIZE
Up to eight children.

TIMING
15 minutes.

ONCE UPON A TIME

Learning objective
To make up their own stories.

What you need
A collection of pictures from magazines, books, catalogues and so on that show a scene with several characters; board; marker pen.

Preparation
Cut out several pictures so that you have a selection to choose from.

What to do
Invite the children to look at the pictures and decide which ones they like the most. When each child has decided on one, look at the pictures in detail together and ask the children to choose one that they all like and to tell you why.

Talk about what they can see in the picture and what is happening. Ask, 'Who do you think this is?', 'Where are they?', 'What are they doing?', 'Where have they been?', 'What are they going to do next?' and so on.

When you have exhausted all possibilities of questions, say, 'Let's make up a story about this picture'. Ask the children for ideas on how to begin the story. If they do not suggest anything, start with 'Once upon a time…'. Invite each child to offer a sentence, describing the characters or the events. When you have been through the whole story once and have a consistent story-line, suggest that you scribe the story for the children. Ask them to help you write it down by telling you what to write. Use shared writing demonstration techniques as you write, asking the children which direction you should write in, what sound some of the words begin with and which word should come next.

Support
Make sure that all the children have the same input when adding sentences to the story.

Extension
Talk about the characters in the story. Ask the children to describe them and to tell you things about them. Suggest using the same characters in another story. Make the new story into a little book and ask the children to illustrate it and give it a title.

HOME LINKS
Encourage the children to take turns to take the story home to read with their carers.

MULTICULTURAL LINKS
Look for pictures that show characters or settings from different cultures to give the story a multicultural influence.

GROUP SIZE
Up to 20 children.

TIMING
15 to 30 minutes.

GRANDAD SAYS...

Learning objective
To use language to imagine and re-create roles and experiences.

What you need
No special equipment.

HOME LINKS
Ask carers to encourage their children to take part in imaginary play at home, such as playing shops, cafés, going to the dentist's and so on.

MULTICULTURAL LINKS
If you are in a multicultural community, ask community leaders to come in to talk to the children about special occasions or festivals. Improvise events from their descriptions, such as going to a Divali party.

What to do
Sit the children in a circle and explain to them that you are going to make up some plays and pretend to be the people in them. Start by giving an example such as 'Grandad says…' and then add a sentence, for example, 'Let's go to the park'. The child next to you should go into the circle and choose two or three children to improvise the role-play. Help the children to think about the things that they might do in the park, for example, go on the playground equipment, walk around the pond, feed the ducks, play with a ball and so on. When you think the improvisation has run its course, ask 'Grandad' to say, 'Let's go home!'. Invite the children to sit down again in the circle.

Encourage the children to suggest another idea to role-play. Be ready with some suggestions in case they are not sure what is expected of them, for example, 'Let's bake some cookies', 'Let's make a snowman', 'Let's build a den in the garden' or 'Let's go fishing'.

When the children have finished role-play, ask them how they felt about 'being' someone else. Did they like the experience? Why?

Support
Some children will find it very hard to improvise in front of the group, while others will 'play to the gallery'. Try to guide the 'choosers' towards a mix of children each time so that no one becomes a 'leader' and anyone who is shy is not missed out. Encourage the shy children by improvising with them.

Extension
Change 'Grandad' to someone very different such as an alien, a friendly giant, a princess and so on, and suggest more complicated actions.

HELLO, HOW ARE YOU?

Learning objective
To interact with others and take turns in conversation.

What you need
Pieces of card; felt-tipped pens; scissors; mobile phone.

Preparation
Cut out a mobile-phone shape for each child from the pieces of card.

What to do
Give each child a card 'mobile phone'. Show them the real mobile phone and ask them if they know what it is for and how it works. Explain that people have conversations on their phones – one person speaks and then the other person speaks. Put the key lock on the mobile phone then pass it around so that the children can see the numbers and symbols on the keys.

Ask the children to draw the different keys on their own 'mobile phones', then write the numbers on the keys for them. Divide the children into pairs and send them to different parts of the room so that they can have conversations with each other using their 'mobile phones'. If the children find it difficult to make conversation, suggest some scenarios that they could improvise, for example, someone calling the doctor or the hospital, someone calling a friend to see how they are, someone calling to order a pizza, someone calling to tell another person their news, someone calling to sell something, and so on.

Observe and listen to the children having their conversations. Suggest that they act out their conversations to other members of the group.

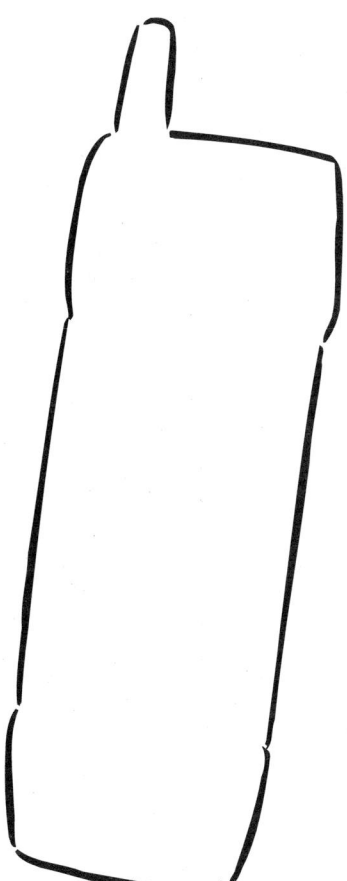

Support
Help the children to make the mobile phones. Be aware of very shy children and assist them with their input into the conversations. Carry out 'mobile phone' conversations with the children.

Extension
During circle time, begin a topic of conversation and encourage the children to take turns to speak.

WHAT HAPPENED NEXT?

Learning objective
To retell narratives in the correct sequence, drawing on the language patterns of stories.

What you need
The children's favourite story-books.

Preparation
Find out several stories that are well known to the children. Familiarize yourself with them.

What to do
As a supply teacher, you are in a prime position for asking the children to retell narratives because you can 'pretend' that you do not know the stories! For each session, choose two or three stories that the children have heard before. Invite them, individually, to tell each story to the group. If the child misses something out and the

other children do not intervene, be ready to give a prompt or cue. Help the children by asking, 'What is the story about?', 'Who is the story about?', 'What happens at the beginning?' and so on. Give the first sentence of the story if you know it, asking, for example, 'Does the story begin something like this…?' and giving the opening.

Make a rule that the other children are only allowed to help if they put up their hand and make their interventions sensibly – they are not allowed to interrupt or shout out.

Encourage the children to use vocabulary such as 'first', 'next', 'and then' and 'in the end' to create the idea of a sequence of events.

Support
Give plenty of encouragement and praise to the children who find it difficult to speak in front of the whole group. Prompt them with appropriate questions such as 'What happened then?', 'Did someone else come along?' or 'How did that happen?'. Help them to verbalize their ideas by speaking quietly with them so that they do not feel threatened in any way.

Extension
Tape-record individual children retelling narratives and keep a collection of their recorded stories for them to listen to.

GROUP SIZE
Up to 20 children.

TIMING
Short periods at any time of the day.

LISTEN CAREFULLY

Learning objective
To hear and say initial sounds in words.

What you need
Toy animals, puppets or dolls that you can give names to.

Preparation
Make up alliterative names for your toys, for example, Rashid Rabbit, Bobby Bear, Dora Doll and so on.

What you do
Sit the children in a circle. Choose one of your props, for example, Bobby Bear. Explain to the children that Bobby Bear has a secret, and they have to listen very carefully to try to find out what it secret is. Tell them that Bobby Bear likes beakers, but he doesn't like cups. Bobby Bear likes bangles, but he doesn't like earrings. Bobby Bear likes books but he doesn't like stories. The idea of the game is for the children to join in when they realize that Bobby Bear likes things that begin with the same sound as his name but doesn't like things that begin with different sounds. The children will most likely focus on the words rather than the sounds so give them plenty of clues by emphasizing the 'b' for 'Bobby', 'bear' and 'beaker'. Point out that Bobby Bear likes beakers and bangles and books and boys and bananas' and so on until they have worked out the secret. When the children have grasped the idea of the game, they should not tell the secret, but add things to the spoken list. If they are correct, give lots of praise; if they are wrong, just say, 'Oh no, Bobby Bear doesn't like … but he does like bananas.'

Play this game with all the initial sounds. Even when the secret has been revealed and the children understand the game, they will still enjoy working out quickly which new sound you are playing with.

HOME LINKS
Encourage carers to play 'I spy' games with the children using sounds instead of letter names while on walks, in the car or at home.

Support
Help the children who may not be able to hear initial sounds clearly. Look out for children who present 'r' as 'w' and 'f' as 's'. Show the children how to make the sounds with the shape of their mouth, but try to work out what the children actually hear because the problems can easily be related to auditory discrimination.

Extension
If the children show signs of knowing letters, move on a stage and encourage them to identify the letter character(s) that match the beginning sound.

GROUP SIZE
Four or five children at a time.

TIMING
30 minutes at a time.

HOME LINKS
Let the children take turns to take the ABC book home to share with their families.

MULTICULTURAL LINKS
When the children are well aware of the English alphabetical concept, explain that some languages use a different alphabet. Try to obtain some alphabet books in a different language for them to look at and compare.

OUR OWN ABC

Learning objective
To link sounds to letters, naming and sounding the letters of the alphabet.

What you need
Fifteen sheets of sugar paper; felt-tipped pens; scissors; glue; stapler; magazines; catalogues; comics.

Preparation
Fold the sheets of sugar paper and staple them together to make a scrapbook. Ensure that the children are aware of the alphabet and have looked at ABC books in previous sessions.

What to do
Tell the children that you are going to make a big ABC book together. Look at some ABC books and talk about the format of the books and what is on the pages. Explain to the children how an ABC book works, saying that each page has a letter of the alphabet in the correct order, and shows things beginning with that letter.

Show the children how to write a capital 'A' and a lower case 'a' on the inside page of the scrapbook and explain the difference between the two letters as you write them.

Ask the children to look through the magazines and catalogues and to find a picture of something beginning with 'a'. Help one child to cut out the chosen item and glue it on to the appropriate page.

Continue until the book is completed. On the first page, write 'Our own ABC' as a title and the name of the group as the 'author'.

Display the book with any published ABC books available to the group. Read through 'Our own ABC' as often as the children will share it with you, and make sure that it is accessible for them to look at whenever they want to.

Support
Help the children to identify items by looking through the pictures with them and saying, 'We are looking for something beginning with "a"', 'What's this?', 'What do you think it is?', 'Do you think it begins with "a"?', 'Shall we cut it out for the book?' and so on.

Extension
Sing the alphabet to the traditional tune and teach it to the children while you point to the letters.

Encourage the children to identify letters that are out of alphabetical order during a few spare minutes.

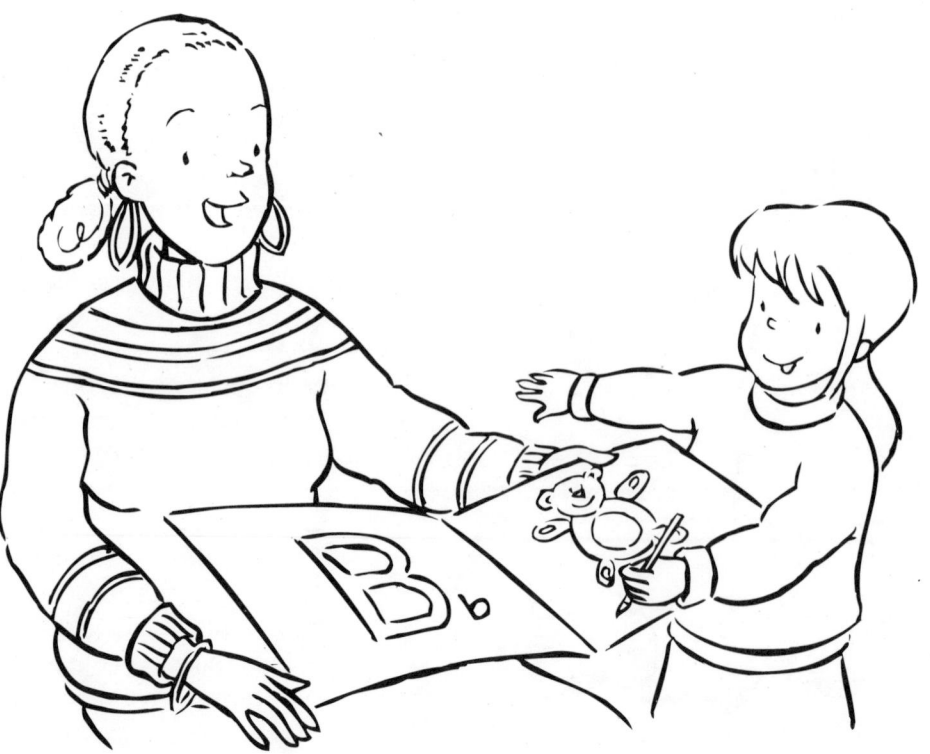

SEND A POSTCARD

Learning objective
To write their own names.

What you need
A cardboard box; blank postcards; pencils; red paper.

Preparation
Make a post-box out of the cardboard box. Cut a hole for posting and cover the whole box with the red paper. Write a collection time on it.

What to do
Talk to the children about their first names. Tell them that it is good to be able to write your own name because you can send messages to other people. Explain that you would like them to send some messages to one another and that you are going to help them to write their own names at the end of their messages.

Give each child a blank postcard. Ask them to decide who they would like to send it to. Show the children how to write 'Dear…, How are you? Love from…' on their postcards and help each child to write their own name at the bottom of their card. Write the recipient's name (another child or adult in the setting) on the other side and invite the senders to post their cards in the post-box. Try to ensure that each child receives a card, writing some yourself if anyone is missed out.

Arrange a collection time when the children are all together. Invite a child to be the postperson collecting the post and giving out the cards. Encourage the rest of the children to help to read who they are to. Give clues such as 'This name begins with "t"' (say the name and the sound of the letter). 'Who do we know whose name begins with a "t"?'. If there are several names beginning with 't', tell the children the next sound and the next, and help them to spell out the name from the auditory clues.

Have a follow-up session when the children can write replies to the first cards. Once again, help them to write their own names, if necessary.

Support
Provide name cards with the children's own names on to help them with their writing.

Extension
Encourage the children to practise writing their own names at every given opportunity, such as on the pictures that they have drawn to take home.

SHOPPING LIST

Learning objective
To attempt writing for different purposes.

What you need
Board; marker pen; paper; pencils.

Preparation
Play the game 'When I went shopping I bought…' where the children add an item to the memory list as you go around the circle, trying to remember everything in the correct order.

What to do
Suggest to the children that it is much easier to remember a lot of things if you write a list for them. Demonstrate writing a list, asking the children for suggestions, for example, a list of names to invite people to a party, or a list of presents that you could buy for a grandparent, or a list of things that you would need to get for a new puppy. Show the children how you write the list with the items one beneath the other.

Gather ideas for a new list that the children could try to write, or play the 'When I went shopping I bought…' game for a few minutes and then ask the children to write as much of the list as they can remember. Encourage them to use their emergent writing skills to attempt the list. Give lots of praise for remembering to write the items one under the other, and for any letter sounds or words that the children get correct. Invite them to read their lists back to you.

Support
Scribe for any children who are not confident to attempt writing the list, asking them, for example, 'What shall I write?', 'Where shall I start?', 'What sound does it begin with?' and 'How do I do that?'. This constant kind of demonstration will help them to absorb knowledge of the skills and confidence to try for themselves.

Extension
Have plenty of paper and pencils available in the various play areas so that the children understand that writing can be an integral part of any activity, particularly making lists when playing in the shopping area.

CHAPTER 3

Use these ideas to help develop the children's understanding of numbers, sizes, patterns, shapes, position and weights. Activities include comparing the size of apples, counting T-shirts, role-playing being aliens and weighing dinosaurs.

Mathematical development

GROUP SIZE
Up to eight children.

TIMING
15 minutes.

HOME LINKS
Ask carers to encourage counting to ten at every opportunity, for example, when going upstairs to bed and downstairs in the morning, cups, dishes and spoons for breakfast, ducks in the bath and so on.

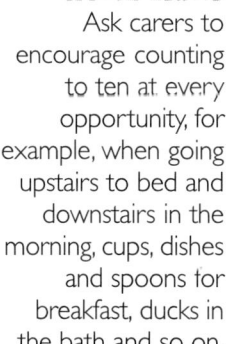

MULTICULTURAL LINKS
Invite carers who are speakers of other languages to teach you and the children to count to ten in their home languages.

LET'S COUNT

Learning objective
To count reliably up to ten.

What you need
A large, open space.

Preparation
Practise some simple actions and movements with the children.

What to do
Sit in a circle with the children and invite them to count to ten with you. Tell them that you are going to play a counting game. They have to take turns to choose a number up to ten and an action for everyone to do.

Demonstrate to the children what they are going to do, for example, say, 'I can nod my head seven times'. Ask the children to count while you nod your head seven times, then ask them to do the same thing while you count with them.

Invite a child to go into the centre of the circle and decide on an activity, for example, clapping. The child says, 'I can clap ten times' (or any number to ten), and claps while the other children count. Then the child asks, 'Can you clap ten times?'. All the children clap while the child counts out loud. Invite another child to choose a different number and a different activity. Suggest activities, for example, jumps, hands up, stand up, sit down, hops, making fists, arm rolls and so on.

Support
Help the children to count slowly, ensuring one-to-one correspondence. Assist the children who find any of the movements difficult by suggesting subtle changes for them.

Extension
Invite the children to play 'Follow-my-leader' and do a chosen number of strides, fairy steps, skips, hops and so on. Count fairly slowly to ensure one-to-one correspondence.

ONE TO NINE

Learning objective
To recognize numerals 1 to 9.

What you need
The photocopiable sheets on pages 72 and 73.

Preparation
Copy the photocopiable sheets on to card and cut out the boxes to provide a set of cards for each child and one for yourself.

What to do
Mix up each set of numeral cards so that the numerals are not in order, and give each child a set. Explain that their numerals have all got into the wrong order and that you are going to help them sort them out. Ask them to spread out their own set in front of them.

Show a card with the numeral 1. Ask the children to find their own number 1 cards. Ask, 'What number is this?' and let them answer, 'It is number 1'. They should then place their cards face up in front of them. Next, show the numeral 2 and repeat the process, putting numeral 2 after numeral 1, so that they are in the correct order. Carry on until you have shown all the numerals and each child has a set, in the correct order, in front of them.

Give each child a set of the dot cards. Hold up one of your own dot cards and ask the children to count the dots and tell you what the numeral should be. Then ask each child to find their own matching dot card and put it with its appropriate matching numeral card. Reinforce the word for each numeral.

Support
Provide plenty of support for the children who find it difficult to count the dots.

Extension
Divide the children into pairs and let them play numeral and/or dot 'Snap', making sure that they verbalize the numerals.

Draw and cut out large numerals for the children to handle, colour in and put into the correct sequence.

GROUP SIZE
Up to six children.

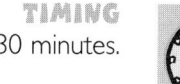

TIMING
30 minutes.

RED AND GREEN APPLES

Learning objective
To use language such as 'smaller than' and 'bigger than'.

What you need
Up to six small pieces of card; long sheet of card; felt-tipped pens; scissors.

Preparation
Draw a different-sized apple on each small piece of card. Make sure that there are clear differences in size.

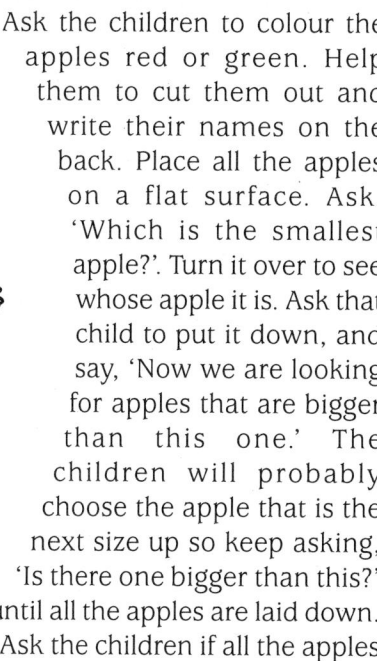

What to do
Ask the children to colour the apples red or green. Help them to cut them out and write their names on the back. Place all the apples on a flat surface. Ask, 'Which is the smallest apple?'. Turn it over to see whose apple it is. Ask that child to put it down, and say, 'Now we are looking for apples that are bigger than this one.' The children will probably choose the apple that is the next size up so keep asking, 'Is there one bigger than this?' until all the apples are laid down. Ask the children if all the apples are bigger than the smallest one. Repeat this process the other way around, starting with the biggest apple and finding apples that are smaller.

Put all the apples on the table and mix them up. Invite a child to take an apple and a second child to take another one. Ask, 'Is Peter's apple bigger or smaller than Rashid's apple?'. Put the first apple back on the table. Ask a third child to take an apple and repeat the question, changing the names as appropriate. Continue doing this until all the children have had a turn.

Support
Help the children who are unsure to compare and contrast books, toys, blocks, hoops and beanbags.

Extension
Glue the apples on to card, in size order, to make a 'Bigger than/smaller than' display.

Alternatively, make a zigzag book. Fold a long piece of card and stick one apple on to each page with text suggested by the children, for example, 'Shazia's apple is bigger than Mark's but it is smaller than Gemma's'.

HOME LINKS
Explain to carers what the children have been doing and ask them to encourage their children to look for 'bigger' and 'smaller' things whenever the opportunity arises.

GROUP SIZE
Five children.

TIMING
20 minutes.

HANG OUT THE T-SHIRTS

Learning objective
To find one less than a number from one to ten.

What you need
The photocopiable sheet on page 74; crayons; scissors; ten easily-manipulated pegs or paper clips; piece of string.

Preparation
Tie the piece of string across a corner of the room or between two chairs to make a clothes line. Make two copies of the photocopiable sheet for each child. Ensure that the children are comfortable with counting from one to ten and with one-to-one correspondence before you carry out this activity.

What you do
Give each child two copies of the photocopiable sheet and ask them to colour the T-shirts, then help them to cut them out. Encourage the children to count with you the number of T-shirts. Invite them to imagine that the T-shirts have been washed and need to be hung on the line.

Choose a child to hang one of their T-shirts on the line. Ask, 'How many T-shirts are left?'. Reinforce the numbers by saying, 'We had ten to start with, we took one away, so how many do we have left?'.

Choose a different child to peg out another T-shirt. Ask, 'How many T-shirts are left now?'. Reinforce the numbers by saying, 'We started with ten T-shirts, we have pegged out two, so how many do we have left?'.

Repeat the process until all the T-shirts are pegged on the line. Count the T-shirts on the line, then pretend that they are dry – so begin the process all over again, taking them off the line! When all the T-shirts have been unpegged, give a small set to one child to count and put the rest of them to one side for the time being. Repeat the processes that you went through with ten T-shirts, but this time with fewer than ten, so that the children can begin to understand that the counting and taking away can start at any number before ten. Repeat with the different number of T-shirts that you have put to one side.

Support
Help the children who are less confident with counting from one to ten and with one-to-one correspondence.

HOME LINKS
Ask carers to play games with their children using a number of objects, taking one away and counting how many are left.

Extension
Encourage the children to estimate the number of T-shirts by taking some away and asking, 'How many do you think are left?'. When the children have decided, count the T-shirts to find the answer. Ask them how many they think will be left if you take another one away and put it with the other set.

GROUP SIZE
Up to five children.

TIMING
15 minutes.

HOME LINKS
Ask carers to send
in any spare pieces
of patterned
wallpaper or fabric
for the children to
explore.

**MULTICULTURAL
LINKS**
Look for traditional
patterns from other
cultures for the
children to
investigate, such as
Islamic tiles or
mendhi patterns.
Ask them to look at
the colours and
shapes and the way
that these move
across the paper or
fabric. Try to
re-create some of
the patterns.

COLOURED PATTERNS

Learning objective
To re-create a simple repeating pattern.

What you need
Large sheet of paper; small tile-shaped coloured stickers.

Preparation
Cut the large sheet of paper into a mathematical shape, such as a circle, or into a random shape, as backing paper.

What to do
Explain to the children that you are going to make a pattern together. Can they tell you how patterns work or what patterns are? Encourage them to use the words 'repeat', 'again' or 'in the same order' when describing patterns. Take some time to investigate how patterns can work through colours, shapes or movements.

Tell the children that the kind of pattern that you are going to make has colours in a certain order, and that when you get to the end of the pattern, the colours start again. Ask the children to suggest what shape the pattern could be, for example, a star, a wheel, a triangle and so on. Draw this shape on to your backing paper.

Encourage the children to help you identify and count the colours of the tiles that you have. Ask, 'Which colour shall we start with?' and 'Where on the shape shall we begin?'. Invite a child to stick the first tile in place. Repeat with different colours until you have used all the colours once. Keep reminding the children that you are making a 'repeating' pattern. Ask, 'Which colour tile needs to be next?' and 'Where should it go?'. Continue until you have covered the shape with the tiles in a repeating pattern. Encourage the children to explain how the pattern works.

Support
Help the children who are less confident with identifying or naming the colours to use matching strategies.

Extension
Provide each of the children with a small piece of paper where you have drawn a line down the centre. Ask them to do random sticking on one side of the line and to match that pattern on the other side, thus creating a repeat. Can they do a second repeat? Can they explain to you how the pattern works?

TRICKY TRIANGLES

Learning objective
To use language to describe the shape and size of 2-D shapes.

What you need
A set of 2-D coloured shapes; large bag.

What you do
Lay the 2-D shapes out flat so that the children can see them easily. Talk about them together, identifying the colours and how many sides they have. Discuss the names of the shapes and help the children to identify each one. Encourage them to use mathematical language such as 'same', 'different', 'corner', 'curve', 'straight', 'point' (angle), 'round' and 'circle'. Collect up all the shapes and put them into the bag.

Explain to the children that they are going to play a game where they can collect points for guessing which shapes are 'tricky triangles'. Pull a shape a little way out of the bag so that just a small section is showing. Suggest a number of points that are on offer, for example, 50. Encourage the children to describe what they can see. Ask them, 'Is it curved?', 'Is it straight?', 'Is it a corner?' and so on. Do they think that it might be a triangle? If they answer no, invite them to tell you why. If they think that the shape is definitely not a triangle, pull it out of the bag to find out. If it is a triangle, then the 'tricky triangle' wins the points. If it is not, the children win the points. Keep going until you have taken out all the 'tricky triangles' from the bag. Decide who wins the game – the children or the 'tricky triangles'!

Support
Keep up a running commentary while the children are playing the game, reminding them that a triangle has three sides and three angles, but that they do not always look the same.

Extension
Cut out some triangles from card, for example, equilateral, right angle, obtuse, acute and so on, to demonstrate to the children the various kinds of triangles and to explore their properties. Make a display of the triangles with a caption reading 'All these shapes are triangles because they have three straight sides and three angles'.

GROUP SIZE
Up to eight children.

TIMING
15 minutes.

WHO'S IN FRONT?

Learning objective
To use everyday words to describe position.

What you need
A different toy for each child such as a bear, doll, dog and so on.

What to do
Sit the children together on the floor and give each child a toy. Invite them to take turns to place their toys in a single line, one behind the other, all facing the same way. Suggest a point to aim at, such as the door or window. Ask, 'Who is in front of the line?' and 'Who is at the end of the line?'.

Invite the children to collect their toys. Put a box where the line of toys was and ask the children, in turn, to place their toys somewhere relating to the box. Ask, 'Who is in front of the box?', 'Who is behind the box?', 'Who is underneath the box?', 'Who is on top of the box?' and so on. Then turn the questions around, saying, for example, 'Tom, where is the doll?'. Choose another child and say, 'Lucy, where is the bear?'. Carry on until all the children have had a turn at describing a position.

Invite the children to collect their toys. Discuss with them all the places that the toys could go in the room. Let each child have a turn to put their toy somewhere, and choose another child to describe where it is. Help them to use the correct positional words.

Ask the children to collect their toys again and give each child an instruction to follow, such as, 'Sanjay, put your toy in front of the books'. When Sanjay has followed the instruction, say, 'Sanjay, tell us where your toy is'.

Support
Be aware of any children with poor language development. Help them to repeat the positional words after you. They will need to hear them and use them at least five times to begin to absorb them.

Extension
When the toys are in a line, encourage the children to describe their positions in terms of first, second, third and so on.

HOME LINKS
Ask carers to encourage their children by using positional words in their normal everyday language, such as when laying the table or pegging out washing.

ALIEN ACTION

Learning objective
To use and say number words in familiar contexts.

What you need
A large, open space.

What to do
Invite the children to find a space where they have got room to move around freely. Tell them that they are going to pretend to be aliens. Describe what aliens are, for example, they could be similar to a robot, made of tin, with a cube-shaped head, straight, tubular arms and straight, tubular legs. The robots' eyes flash and their bodies move in a jerky way. Explain that robots have come from Number and Shape Land and have landed on Earth. They are looking for anything that they recognize such as numbers, shapes, patterns, opportunities to count and build, and so on. Encourage the children to practise some robot movements.

Invite a child to be the leader of the aliens. Ask them to carry out some actions and describe what they are doing, for example, 'We are going in a straight line', 'We can see five toys', 'We have found a round bin', 'We are going along a curvy pathway' and so on. After a few minutes, change the leader, to give everyone a chance to lead.

Ask the 'aliens' to sit down and to tell you what they think Number and Shape Land might be like. Ask, 'Is it square?', 'Is it round?', 'Has it got numbers instead of trees?', 'What shape are the houses?', 'Do the aliens only eat shapes?' and so on. Encourage the children to use their imagination and as much mathematical language as they possibly can.

Divide the children into two groups to role-play being the aliens from Number and Shape Land, arriving in your environment and seeing it for the first time.

Support
Some of the children might be reluctant to take a turn as the leader. Help them to think of movements and actions and verbalize to the others what they are doing.

Extension
Discuss the children's ideas about Number and Shape Land. Invite them to draw or paint pictures of the aliens and some of the things that they might see there. Stick the pictures to a background to make a display of the aliens moving in a straight line in Number and Shape Land, as well as moving in a circle or a curved line.

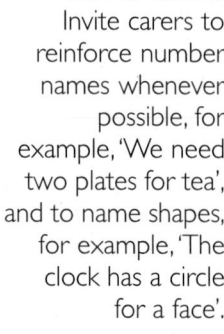

GROUP SIZE
Ten children.

TIMING
Ten minutes.

HERE COMES ANOTHER ONE!

Learning objective
To find one more than a number from one to ten.

What you need
A large, open space.

What to do
Invite the children to stand in a space and pretend to be elephants. Hold one arm out in front of you as the elephant's trunk and show the children how the elephant moves – plod, plod, plod, waving his trunk from side to side. Describe how elephants sometimes move in a 'Follow-my-leader' line.

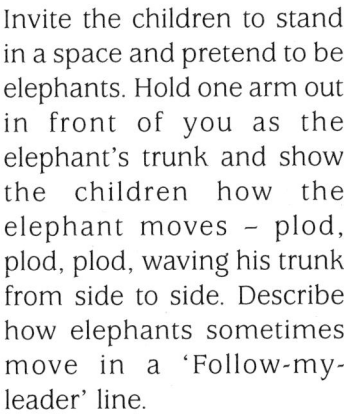

Invite the children to use one hand in front of them as a trunk and one hand behind them as a tail. Encourage each elephant to curl its trunk around the tail of the elephant in front (the children should hold hands to join the trunks and tails).

Tell the children that you are going to play an 'adding-on' elephant game. Invite an enthusiastic child to stand up and pretend to be the first elephant. Tell the 'elephant' to listen carefully to the story that you are going to tell and do what the elephant is doing. Make up a simple story starting with, 'There is one elephant who goes to the side of the pond to have a drink and then along comes another one'. Choose another 'elephant' to join the first one. Ask the children, 'How many elephants are there now?'.

Continue the story with the elephants drinking and squirting, standing up tall and lying down on their front legs, and catching each other's tails in their trunks, with more and more elephants joining in, until there are ten.

Support
Ensure that the children are happy with the concept of 'elephant'. Discuss the characteristics of an elephant before they begin the role-play, for example, how big they are, how heavy they are, how big their feet are, how they move, where they live, and so on.

Extension
Invite the children to pretend to be penguins, kangaroos, lions and so on. Ask, 'If there are six elephants and the next animal to come along is a lion, or a penguin, does it change the number of animals?'.

HOME LINKS
Explain to carers that the children are working on 'adding one'. Ask them to let their children help when they are counting out plates, dishes, cups and so on for meals at home, or working out how many biscuits there should be so that there is one for everyone.

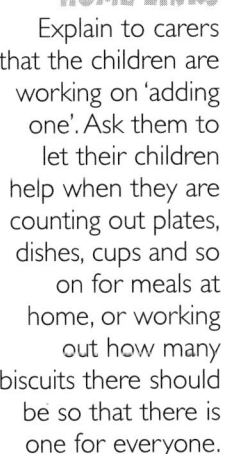

MULTICULTURAL LINKS
Look for simple reference books showing Indian and African elephants in their natural habitats, and share them with the children.

GROUP SIZE
Four children at a time.

TIMING
Five to ten minutes.

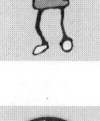

WEIGH THE DINOSAURS

Learning objective
To use language such as 'heavier than' and 'lighter than'.

What you need
The photocopiable sheet on page 75; scissors; crayons; Plasticine; Lego bricks; paper; card; coins; paper clips; sticky tape; weighing scales; felt-tipped pen.

Preparation
Make several copies of the photocopiable sheet.

What to do
Give each child a copy of the photocopiable sheet and ask them to cut out the dinosaur carefully and then to colour it in. If necessary, cut out the dinosaurs for the children. Invite a child to choose an object such as a coin, Lego brick or paper clip to tape to the back of their dinosaur. When the objects have been attached, ask the children to predict which dinosaur will be the heaviest, which will be the lightest, whether Ben's will be heavier than Jamila's, and so on. Ask the children to give reasons for their predictions. They will probably think that the dinosaur with the biggest object stuck to it will be the heaviest, and the one with the smallest will be the lightest, so emphasize to them that this is not necessarily so.

Use the scales to find out which object is the heaviest and so on. Encourage each child to verbalize how heavy their dinosaur is in comparison to the others – for example, 'Emma's elephant is heavier than Charlotte's, but not as heavy as Rashid's'.

Give each child another two dinosaurs and encourage them to decide whether they should make the second dinosaur heavier or lighter than the first one, and so on. Invite them to stick objects to them and then use the scales to see if they have predicted correctly.

Support
Provide younger children with plenty of assistance when taping to their dinosaurs the objects that they have chosen.

Extension
Encourage the children to write their predictions on a chart with two columns, one headed 'Predictions for heaviest dinosaur' and the other 'Predictions for lightest dinosaur'. Add objects to the dinosaurs to explore what will make the lightest one the heaviest, and take objects off the heaviest one to see how light it can be made.

HOME LINKS
Explain to carers that the children have been comparing weights. Encourage them to involve their children when they are weighing items in cooking, and to talk about 'heavier' and 'lighter'.

CHAPTER 4

Knowledge and understanding of the world

Encourage the children to find out about their surroundings and be aware of the things around them with the following activities. Ideas include using toys to look at similarities, compare differences in animals, have a 'show and tell' session and use the outdoor area to explore the natural world.

GROUP SIZE
Up to six children.

TIMING
30 minutes.

HOME LINKS
Ask carers to help their children to explore their immediate environment at home and, perhaps, keep a notebook of drawings of different species of animals or plants that are common in their surroundings.

MULTICULTURAL LINKS
Be aware of any specific cultural preferences or rejections of certain species that could arise.

LET'S EXPLORE

Learning objective
To find out about their immediate environment.

What you need
The photocopiable sheet on page 76; magnifying glass; pencils.

Preparation
Make a copy of the photocopiable sheet for each child.

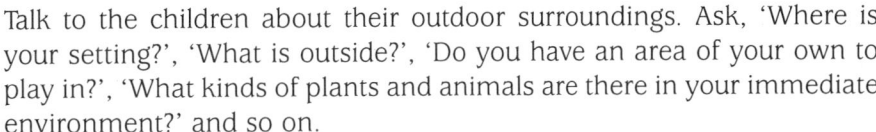

What to do
Talk to the children about their outdoor surroundings. Ask, 'Where is your setting?', 'What is outside?', 'Do you have an area of your own to play in?', 'What kinds of plants and animals are there in your immediate environment?' and so on.

Take the children outdoors to explore. Encourage them to look for plant life, for example, flowers, bushes, trees, weeds and so on, and animal life such as ants, birds, beetles, butterflies, flies and so on. Identify the different species and name them for the children. Invite the group to look in detail and to verbally describe what they can see, using the magnifying glass if necessary. Encourage the children to use their sense of hearing as well as sight. Ask, 'What can you hear?'.

When you return indoors, give each child a copy of the photocopiable sheet and a pencil, and ask them to draw one plant and one animal that they have seen outdoors. Scribe for them or help them to use emergent writing skills to write a caption for each picture.

Support
Help the children to remember what they saw outdoors by asking questions such as, 'How many legs did the beetle have?', 'What colour were the butterfly's wings?', 'Was the sparrow bigger or smaller than the pigeon?' and so on.

Extension
Collect some reference books and help the children to look for the same or similar species by pointing out similarities and differences.

LIVING OR NOT LIVING?

Learning objective
To identify some features of living things.

What you need
Flip chart; felt-tipped pen.

What to do
Sit the children in a circle. Tell them that you are going to discuss how we know whether something is 'living' or 'not living'. Invite them to name some things that they think are living. How do they know? Ask them to name some things that they think are not living. How do they know?

Make a list of things that 'living' things do that 'non-living' things do not do. Use people as an example and ask the children to tell you how we know that we are living – for example, we grow, breathe, eat, drink, move, have babies and so on. Other living things share most, if not all, of these faculties. Invite the children to suggest other things that are living and check off the criteria as you discuss them. Ask for some examples of non-living things and check off the criteria again.

Support
Be aware of any children who may have experienced bereavement of a family member or pet. They will often want to talk about death. Respond sensitively, but explain that, in a way, dying is part of living and that when you ask for things that are 'not living', you mean things that have never been alive.

HOME LINKS
Explain to carers
that you have been
discussing living and
non-living things,
and ask them to
help their children
to decide on items
that they see on the
way home.

Extension
Invite each child to draw and colour something that is living and something that is not living. Help them to cut out their pictures. Make a small book and stick a living thing on one page and a non-living thing on the opposite page until you have used all the pictures. Ask each child to identify their pictures, and scribe for them or help them to use emergent writing skills to write a caption for each picture. Give the book a title and the children's names as authors.

PET ANIMALS

Learning objective
To find out about living things.

What you need
Photographs of any pets that you may have, or pictures of domestic animals.

What to do
Sit the children where they are comfortable for discussion. Tell them that you are going to talk about pets. Remind them of the rules for talking to the group – you will ask one person at a time to speak and the children should not all try to speak at the same time.

Show the children the photographs and pictures and talk to them about pets. Ask them to put up their hands if they have a pet at home, then invite them to take turns to talk. Guide them to tell the group about their pets. Ask, 'What is your pet?', 'What is its name?', 'How old is it?', 'How long have you had it?', 'Where does it live?', 'Who looks after it?', 'What does it eat?', 'Does its home have to be cleaned out?', 'How do you clean its home?', 'How do you keep your pet clean?', 'What does your pet do?', 'Does it play?', 'What do you think is the best thing about your pet? Why?' and so on.

When you have exhausted most of the discussion, help the children to count how many dogs, cats, rabbits, hamsters, fish and so on the children have between them.

Support
Invite individual children to stand close to you while they are talking to the group. Give reluctant children lots of praise and assist them in verbalizing. Be aware of any children who do not have pets who might feel left out. Be ready to ask them what sort of pet they would choose if they were going to have one, how they would look after it and so on.

Extension
Invite the children to draw and paint pictures of their pets. Scribe for them or help them to use emergent writing skills to write the animals' names. Make a folder from card or sugar paper and label it 'How many pets?'. Punch a hole in the top left-hand corner of the folder and pictures. Thread with a piece of string or ribbon and hang the folder from a hook or drawing pin for everyone to enjoy.

SOFT AND CUDDLY

Learning objective
To look closely at similarities.

What you need
A selection of toys such as soft animals, cars and so on.

What to do

Sit in a circle with the children, the toys in front of you. Explain that you are going to try to sort the toys into groups or sets, and that the only way that you can do this is to decide what is the same about different toys.

Choose two toys, for example, a soft-toy bear and a soft-toy dog. Encourage each child to look at the toys and decide if there is anything that is the same about them. Ask the children what they can tell you about their similarities, for example, they are both cuddly, they are both blue, they both have two eyes, they both have clothes on, and so on. If there are plenty of similarities, put the two toys together in one space and give them a group identification, for example, 'soft toys'.

Pass around another toy, for example, a car. Ask appropriate questions such as, 'Has it got anything the same as the other two toys?', 'Is it cuddly?', 'Is it blue?', 'Does it have two eyes?', 'Is it wearing clothes?' and so on. If the toy is the same colour as the other two, ask the children if they would like to put it into the same group or whether it needs to be put into a different one. They may answer that it could go into the same group but the name of the group would need to be changed to 'blue toys' – this is perfectly acceptable. However, the children may decide to stick to their first criteria and put this toy into a different group, perhaps called 'toys with wheels'. Carry on until you have covered most of the toys and have separated them into organized groups.

Support
If the children point out differences rather than similarities, try to dissuade them by telling them that at the moment you are only looking for things that are the same.

Extension
Gather another selection of toys. Make four groups in the middle of the circle, for example, square things, yellow things, soft things and wheeled things. Give each child a toy from outside your selection. Ask them to look for a similarity between their toy and the toys in the four groups, and to decide which group it should join. Invite them to verbalize their reason and tell the group in which way it is the same. If none of the toys meet the criteria, begin a group of 'things that are not the same'.

GROUP SIZE
Up to six children.

TIMING
20 minutes.

NAME THAT ANIMAL

Learning objective
To look closely at differences.

What you need
The photocopiable sheet on page 78.

Preparation
Make a copy of the photocopiable sheet for each child.

What to do
Give each child a copy of the photocopiable sheet. Encourage them to tell you what they can see on it. Invite them to identify and name the animals, and give them opportunities to verbally describe these. Tell them that you are going to look closely together at the animals on the sheet and try to decide what differences you can see, or discuss the ones that the children already know.

Encourage the children to look at the size of the animals, their skin or coat, their markings, their shape, their feet, their faces, noses and ears, their tails (if any) and other features.

HOME LINKS
Give each child a copy of the photocopiable sheet on page 79 to take home. Explain to carers that you have been looking at 'differences' and ask them to help their children complete the photocopiable sheet.

Ask the children if they know where the animals live, what kind of habitat they prefer, what food they eat, what eats them and what group they belong to – for example, reptile, insect or mammal. Encourage the children to talk about any specific behaviour patterns that the animals might have – for example, the giraffe feeds on leaves and twigs, which it pulls down from trees. Talk about how they move, what kinds of noises they make and how they protect themselves from predators.

Some of the children may have quite a lot of knowledge about different animals, so encourage them to share this with the group. Let them colour the pictures on the photocopiable sheet, and scribe for them or help them to use emergent writing skills to write the name of each animal.

Support
Help the children to look at specific parts of the animals to compare them – for example, they might look at two of the animals' faces and describe the differences between them.

MULTICULTURAL LINKS
Talk about various cultures and how people celebrate different festivals, write in different ways and wear different clothes for special occasions.

Extension
Invite the children to choose two more animals that are very different from each other, paint pictures of them and then verbalize the differences. Help them by looking through reference books or picture books together and talking through the differences before they start to paint.

GROUP SIZE
Up to six children.

TIMING
20 minutes.

HOME LINKS
Make a display of the children's pictures and rubbings, together with some of the objects that the children have examined. Ask carers if they have any interesting patterned items at home that you may borrow to show the children for them to copy and add to the display.

MULTICULTURAL LINKS
Collect some reference books that show traditional patterns and discuss their similarities and differences with the children.

SWIRLY, SPOTTY, STRIPY

Learning objective
To look closely at patterns.

What you need
A collection of familiar, patterned objects such as leaves, stones, tree bark and petals; pictures of patterned animals; paper; pencils.

What to do
Put all the objects and pictures on a table and invite the children to look at them. Point out the patterns and encourage the children to notice any features that are the same and any aspects that are different. Ask each child, in turn, to choose one of the objects or pictures and to describe the pattern to you. Encourage them to use words such as 'straight', 'zigzaggy', 'swirly', 'spotty' and 'stripy'. Ask them to find things that have a similar pattern. Can they think of other things that have similar patterns that they have seen somewhere else? Let the children sort the patterns into similarity groups so that you have sets of straight, round, swirly and spotty patterns and so on.

Invite each child to choose their favourite patterned object or picture. Provide paper and pencil and ask them to draw their chosen pattern on the paper. Scribe for them or help them to use emergent writing skills to write a caption for the pattern, such as 'Ranjit's pattern is a swirly pattern' or 'Sophie's pattern is spotty'.

Support
If the patterns are not very clear and the children are unsure of them, be ready to demonstrate with your fingers, following the lines so that the children can see them.

Extension
Look for items that have a textured pattern on them. Take rubbings using wax crayons. Invite each child to show their rubbing to the group and describe it. Can the other children guess what the rubbing is of?

SHOW AND TELL

Learning objective
To find out about present events in their own lives.

What you need
Items brought in by the children.

Preparation
Invite the children to bring in things that are relevant to their present lives, for example, birthday cards, birthday presents, special toys, special festival cards or photographs of special occasions. Tell the children that if they have something special that they would like to 'show and tell', they should give it to you at the beginning of the session so that you can keep it 'safe' for them. (This will enable you to be prepared for who will be doing the 'showing and telling'.) If any of the children have something to 'tell' but not 'show', for example, a new baby or a visit, then they should also let you know.

GROUP SIZE
Up to ten children.

TIMING
Ten to 15 minutes.

HOME LINKS

Prior to the activity, explain to carers that you would like to have a 'show and tell' session where the children tell the group what is new in their lives, so that they begin to think about time and change. Ask them to give the children some ideas to bring to the group.

MULTICULTURAL LINKS

Be aware of multicultural festivals and encourage the children of different religions to take a full part in the 'show and tell' sessions.

What to do
Set up a 'show and tell' session at a specific time each day. Tell the children that they should sit quietly and listen carefully to the child who is showing and telling.

When the children are ready to be receptive, invite the first child to stand by you to show what they have brought and to tell the rest of the group why they have brought it and what is interesting about it. Ask questions such as, 'Why is it special?', 'What do you like about it?', 'What does it do?' and so on. Give lots of praise and encouragement. If it is appropriate, ask the children at the end of the 'show and tell' to give the child a clap as they sit down.

Support
Some children may need to talk about unhappy family events. Be sensitive to their needs and be aware of their feelings and level of understanding. Guide the group to show regard and understanding for the child's predicament.

Extension
Create role-play activities to help the children reflect upon personal events in their lives, where some of the children can act out an enormous adventure that is happening in someone's life, or a pretend party to celebrate someone's birthday.

NATURAL DISCOVERY

Learning objective
To find out about the natural world.

What you need
An outdoor area; the photocopiable sheet on page 80; sticky tape; pencils.

Preparation
Make a copy of the photocopiable sheet for each child.

What to do
Explain to the children that you are going to go outdoors to look for 'natural' things, not things that might have been 'made'. Ensure that they have an understanding of 'natural' and 'made' materials by asking them to give you some examples of 'natural' things, such as leaves, twigs, feathers, stones, minibeasts, snails and flowers, and 'made' things, such as milk-bottle tops, bits of plastic, paper, cans and flowerpots.

Tell the children that you would like them to find small, natural things to collect. If they see any minibeasts, they can observe them, but they must not collect them. When outdoors, direct the children to an environment where there is some greenery such as a garden or park, or even a small stretch of grass and weed. Help each child to collect four small items and look for any animal life to observe.

Back indoors, talk about what you have seen and what the children have collected. Give each child a copy of the photocopiable sheet and help them to tape their four items in the spaces provided. Scribe for them or help them to use emergent writing skills to label their collection. Invite them to draw a minibeast that they might have observed in the last space.

Help each child to decide on their favourite item, and scribe for them or help them to use emergent writing skills to fill in the last part of the photocopiable sheet. Ensure that the children wash their hands when they have finished touching the objects.

Support
Help the children to decide which things are natural and which are not when they are collecting items outdoors.

Extension
Create a nature table, showing the children's collections and adding other bits and pieces that you have found. Identify the items and scribe for the children or help them to use emergent writing skills to make a label for each item.

GROUP SIZE
Up to eight children.

TIMING
30 minutes at a time.

SPACE SHUTTLE

Learning objective

To select the tools they need to shape, assemble and join the materials they are using.

What you need

Different-sized cardboard boxes; large sheets of corrugated cardboard; foil; card cylinders; empty washing-up-liquid bottles; cotton reels; buttons; scissors; glue sticks; glue pots; glue spreaders; stapler; sticky tape; parcel tape; Blu-Tack; elastic bands; hammer; nails; screws; string; paper clips; whiteboard; marker pen.

Preparation

Lay the materials out where they can be easily seen and are accessible to the children.

What to do

Tell the children that you are going to make a space shuttle that will need to be big enough for two astronauts to sit in it comfortably and have lots of controls. Allow plenty of time for the children to put their ideas together.

Ask the children to share their ideas with you, and try to come to an agreement of what the space shuttle will look like. If the children have a clear idea, draw a picture of it on the board so that everyone knows what they are aiming for.

Start with a large cardboard box as the cabin part that the astronauts will sit in, and use some corrugated cardboard to make a large rocket shape to stick to the front of the cabin. The children will need to decide how to make this and how to join all the pieces together. Encourage them to think of ideas of how to use the foil to show that the rocket is metallic. Discuss each stage of the proceedings and let various children try different ideas to see if they work.

Once the main parts are assembled, concentrate on where the controls will go and how they will need to be put together and joined on to the main part of the space shuttle. Give each child responsibility for making some part of the controls and encourage them to make an independent choice of tools. Remember that at this stage the children need to be experimenting with 'fixing things' and should be allowed to 'get it wrong'. When the space shuttle is finished, talk through the processes that the children used, paying attention to where some of the choices went wrong and why, and then how those problems were overcome.

Support

Be aware of the children whose hand–eye co-ordination or fine motor skills are not as developed as others', and give them plenty of encouragement and help.

Extension

Use the space shuttle for role-play activities and for creating imaginative stories and rhymes.

HOME LINKS
Invite carers in to look at the space shuttle and ask them to discuss their own ideas for refinements with the children.

GROUP SIZE
Four children.

TIMING
Five to ten minutes.

WHAT'S THAT SMELL?

Learning objective

To investigate objects and materials by using all of their senses as appropriate.

What you need

A variety of aromatic items such as an orange, a banana, cheese, different-flavoured crisps, tomato ketchup, a flower, furniture polish and air freshener.

What to do

Have a discussion to find out what the children know about their five senses. Guide them towards naming the senses – seeing, smelling, tasting, feeling and hearing. Ask them if they need to have all five senses working together in order to find out what things are. Why?

Explain to the children that they are going to concentrate on just one sense – the sense of smell. What kind of things can they normally smell? How many good smells can they think of? How many bad smells can they think of?

Tell the children that you have some items that you think they will be able to recognize by just smelling. Ask them to close their eyes tightly, smell and see if they can recognize the items. Emphasize that they must keep their eyes shut – no peeping! Give each child a brief opportunity to smell the first item and remind them not to shout out what they think it is. Put the item out of sight, then ask them to open their eyes. Ask each child in turn to say what they thought the item was. Show the children the item. Were they right or wrong? Give them a 'point' each for getting it right. Do the same with the rest of the items and add up the points.

Support

Be ready for any children who want to tell you of someone that they know who has sense impairment, and respond sensitively.

Extension

Focus on a different sense. For example, make a 'feely bag' with objects inside that the children can touch and identify, or have a hearing session where you play a tape of different everyday sounds and the children can listen and identify them.

HOME LINKS
Ask carers to help their children develop all of their senses by observing and identifying different kinds of texture, sound, smell and taste, wherever possible, rather than just focusing, as we all do much of the time, on vision.

MULTICULTURAL LINKS
Talk about foods from different countries and try to obtain some samples for the children to smell.

CHAPTER 5

Physical development

Concentrate on the children's physical skills, encouraging them to move with confidence, imagination, control and co-ordination, develop an awareness of space, be aware of their own bodies and handle tools with increasing control. Ideas include moving like animals, playing a shadow game and making sandwiches.

GROUP SIZE
Up to 25 children.

TIMING
20 minutes.

LET'S GO!

Learning objective
To move with confidence.

What you need
A safe space, indoors or outdoors, with enough room for the children to be able to stretch their arms wide and turn around on the spot without touching anyone else. (If space is limited, split the children into smaller groups.)

What to do
Help the children to get changed into their PE clothes. To gain control before reaching your movement space, ask the children to form a 'Follow-my-leader' line behind you. Lead them in a slow and rhythmic way so that you have a calm, controlled atmosphere to begin with. Ask the children to find a space and then stand on tiptoes.

Clap a rhythm to which the children can tiptoe to an open space and then back to their own spaces. Tell them that you would like them to tiptoe in and out, and around one another, without touching anyone else. When you clap, they should stay still. When the children can tiptoe around one another with confidence, change the movement to different kinds of travelling, for example, marching, hopping, dancing, striding and so on. Continue to give directions such as 'Move this way and that, make sure that you cannot touch anyone, go in and out, move from space to space'.

Take the children back to their own spaces and ask them to each curl up into a little ball to calm down. Invite them, one by one, to form the 'Follow-my-leader' line, tiptoeing back to your room.

Support
Some children may find it difficult to stay focused on quiet, slow movements and on being still. Be prepared to be quite firm with them in order for the movement session not to descend into chaos, and praise them when they are working as you want them to.

Extension
Play 'Follow-my-leader' games with the children. Lead them, carrying out different actions such as shuffling and turning your arms as the wheels of a train; plodding with your arms held up with sharp claws as a monster; tiptoeing with spiky hands and feet as Jack Frost and so on. When the children have absorbed the rules of staying in line and not overtaking, invite individuals to be the leader.

HOME LINKS
Encourage the children to show their carers how well they can move when they come to collect them.

GROUP SIZE
Up to 25 children.

TIMING
20 minutes.

I AM A MOUSE

Learning objective
To move with imagination.

What you need
A large, open space.

What to do
Ask the children to form a 'Follow-my-leader' line behind you. Lead them in a slow and rhythmic way so that you have a calm, controlled atmosphere to begin with, and ask them to find a space. Tell them that they are going to use their imagination to pretend to be different animals and show you how they can move. Explain that no one must touch anyone else and that they must remain quiet and stay still when you clap your hands.

Start with some quiet kinds of movements, for example, a mouse. Say, 'I am a mouse', and make a 'mouse shape' with a little pinched face, hunched shoulders and 'paws' up. Encourage the children to each pretend to be a mouse, and ask how they will move. They should demonstrate moving in small, quick footsteps. Remind them that you would like them to move this way and that, in and out, around and about, without touching. When they are ready, let them move, and then clap for them to stand still. Ask for suggestions for another animal. Say, 'I am a wallaby' and repeat the activity. Carry on until you have exhausted the children's ideas.

Take the children back to their own spaces and ask them to each curl up into a ball to calm down. Invite them, one by one, to form the 'Follow-my-leader' line, tiptoeing back to your room.

Support
Once the children start to be 'animals', they will probably want to make animal noises. If this gets uncontrollable, tell the children that the animals must move around silently in case a predator hears them and tries to creep up on them.

Extension
Invite individual children to choose an animal and demonstrate to the rest of the group how it might move.

HOME LINKS
Ask carers to share animal reference books with their children and talk with them about how the different creatures move.

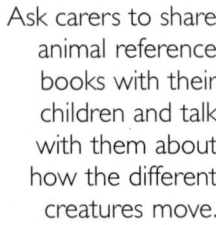

MULTICULTURAL LINKS
Look for pictures of animals from different parts of the world and discuss them with the children.

GROUP SIZE
Up to 25 children.

TIMING
20 minutes.

LOOK AT ME!

Learning objective
To move with control and co-ordination.

What you need
A large, open space.

What to do
Ask the children to form a 'Follow-my-leader' line behind you. Lead them in a slow and rhythmic way so that you have a calm, controlled atmosphere to begin with. Invite each child to find a space, then to find a partner and sit down.

Explain to the children that they are going to play a shadow game, where one child leads and their partner copies.

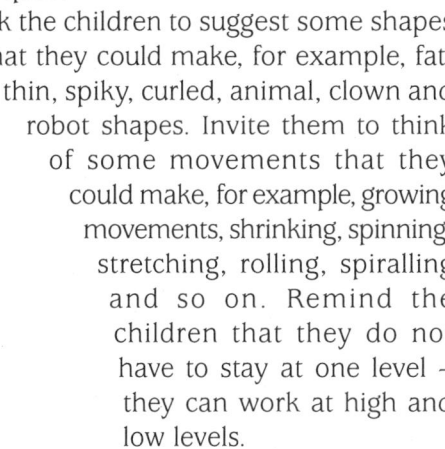

Ask the children to suggest some shapes that they could make, for example, fat, thin, spiky, curled, animal, clown and robot shapes. Invite them to think of some movements that they could make, for example, growing movements, shrinking, spinning, stretching, rolling, spiralling and so on. Remind the children that they do not have to stay at one level – they can work at high and low levels.

Encourage the children to practise moving and copying their partners with lots of control. After a while, ask them to swap over so that the second child has a chance to lead. Invite some of the children to demonstrate their ideas to the rest of the group.

At the end of the session, ask the children to go back to their own spaces and curl up to calm down, then lead them quietly back to your room

Support
If the children are unsure of what is expected of them, choose a child to be your partner and lead them to copy you through some movements and shapes.

Extension
Tell the children that you are going to play 'Statues'. Give them directions for moving around the room and tell them that when you clap your hands you would like them to 'freeze' into any shape that they want and to balance for a few moments, until you clap your hands again, signalling that they can move again.

HOME LINKS
Encourage carers to help their children to explore body shapes and move in different directions.

GROW AND SHRINK

Learning objective
To show awareness of space, of themselves and of others.

What you need
Large, open space; tambour, drum or other instrument that can be beaten.

What to do
Invite the children to each find a space where they can turn around with their arms wide out, without touching anyone else. Explain that they are going to grow and shrink into different shapes and sizes. Encourage them to shrink as slowly as they can to the smallest size that they can possibly be. When they are curled up as tightly as they can, tell them that when you beat the tambour they should begin to grow. They must listen to the rhythm of the beats as this will tell them how fast or slow to move. Beat the tambour very slowly, giving the children time to uncurl themselves as slowly as possible. Remind them that they should grow into a big shape. Keep up a commentary of praise about their control and the shapes that they are making. Encourage them to puff out their tummies and cheeks and stretch other parts of their bodies that they can think of to make them big.

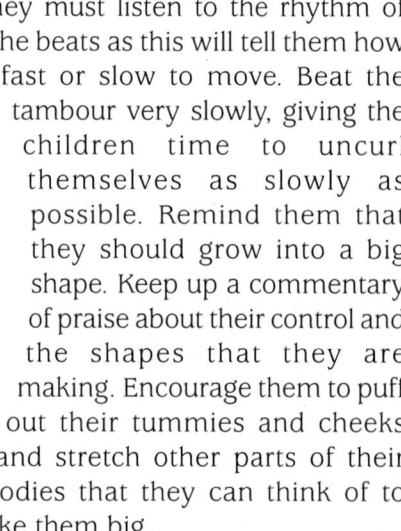

When the children are as big as they can be, ask them to hold their shapes and balance for a few seconds. Tell them that the next time you beat the tambour, you would like them to shrink back down to their curled-up shapes as quickly possible.

Next, ask the children to grow quickly and give them a few moments to travel in any direction they can, holding their big shapes, without touching anyone else. Encourage them to hold their shapes again, then beat the tambour to lead them to shrink very, very slowly.

Support
Encourage the children with lots of praise. Ask questions to make them think about all the parts of their bodies, for example, 'Are your cheeks puffed out as much as they can be?', 'Are your fingers stretched out as far as possible?', 'Are your toes curled up as much as possible?' and so on.

Extension
Invite the children to carry out the activity with another part of their body as well as with their feet on the floor. Encourage them to think about how they can grow in other directions at different levels.

TIMING
Ten to 15 minutes.

STRETCH OUT

Learning objective
To recognize the things which contribute to a healthy body.

What you need
A large, open space; tambour or drum.

What to do
Lead the children into the movement space and invite them to sit down. Ask them what they think are the important things that they can do with their bodies, for example, move, grow and stretch. Focus on stretching. Ask the children which parts of their bodies they think they can stretch. Can they stretch their fingers? Can they stretch their toes? Can they stretch their faces? Can they stretch their legs and their arms? Encourage them to experiment and demonstrate these stretches.

Invite each child to find a space to play a stretching game. Ask them to stretch out both arms in front of them and pretend to be the wide jaws of a crocodile. Encourage them to move around the large space to a strong beat of the tambour, striding, and opening and closing their jaw arms. Then, ask them to move back to a space.

Invite the children to hold up their arms in the air, stretch them as high as they can and pretend to be the long neck of a giraffe. Explain how their hands at the top are the giraffe's mouth, opening and closing to feed on leaves from the tops of the trees. Play a slow but gentle beat for the 'giraffes' to move gracefully around and collect their food. Then ask each child to move back into a space.

When you have finished, lead the children quietly back to your room.

Support
Remind the children to stretch and stretch as much as they possibly can, even while they are moving. Their stretches will probably relax while they are concentrating on their movements, so keep reminding them that they are a crocodile or a giraffe – this will help them to focus on their stretches.

HOME LINKS
Invite carers to
watch the children
doing imaginative
stretching
movements.

Extension
Make up a story about Jack Frost where the children begin as little lumps of snow or water, and then stretch their bodies as the temperature gets colder and colder until they turn into an icy Jack Frost. Encourage them to stretch as much as they possibly can in all directions and make themselves spiky.

GROUP SIZE
Up to ten children.

TIMING
Ten minutes.

GET READY!

Learning objective
To handle a ball with increasing confidence.

What you need
A medium-sized soft ball for each child.

What to do
Ask the children to sit on the floor in a large circle with their legs wide open so that they are forming two sides of a triangle. Kneel on one edge of the circle with one ball.

Tell the children that you are going to roll the ball towards them, one at a time, and that they should try to stop the ball with their hands as it comes into their 'triangle'. Say, 'I am going to roll the ball to Hannah. Get ready!' and roll the ball gently along the floor towards the child. Move around the circle and make sure that everybody has at least two or three turns with you rolling the ball. Give each child an opportunity to be the ball roller.

Divide the children into pairs and give one ball to each pair. The partners should sit opposite each other, not too far from each other, with their legs wide open, and roll the ball, gently, backwards and forwards to each other, saying 'Get ready!' as they roll it.

Next, invite each child to find a space on their own and sit down. Give them a ball and ask them to throw it gently, not very high, into the air and to try to catch it. Explain to them the link between watching the ball and having their hands ready to do the catching, so that they begin to understand the concept of hand–eye co-ordination.

Support
If the children find it difficult to throw and catch the ball, gently throw the ball to them so that they just have to concentrate on catching it.

Extension
Line up several cardboard boxes or tubs. Ask the children to stand approximately one metre away and throw the balls into the boxes. Move the boxes closer or further away as appropriate. Encourage each child to count how many times out of ten throws they can get their ball into the box.

HOME LINKS
Suggest to carers that they play simple ball games, such as 'Skittles' or throwing a ball into a box, with their children at home.

GROUP SIZE
Up to ten children.

TIMING
Ten to 15 minutes.

MAKE A TUNNEL

Learning objective
To travel under and over equipment.

What you need
Large cardboard boxes; parcel tape.

What to do
Show the children the cardboard boxes and suggest that they help you to make a tunnel with them. Undo both ends of each box and fix all the boxes together with parcel tape to make one long tunnel.

Invite the children to travel through the tunnel in different ways, for example, crawling on their tummies, squatting, bumping on their bottoms, crawling on their hands and knees, shuffling on their bottoms, creeping commando style by pulling themselves along by their arms, and so on.

When the children have explored all opportunities for travelling under the tunnel, suggest that you make it into something to climb over. Collapse the boxes along one of the sides to make a triangular shape instead of a square shape.

Ask the children to find different ways of travelling over the collapsed tunnel, for example, crawling and sliding on their tummies, sliding on their bottoms, climbing, rolling, pulling themselves over with their arms, climbing and jumping, and so on.

Support
Be ready to help any children who are not very confident in their physical abilities, to ensure that they do not tumble.

Extension
Talk to the children about tunnels. Ask them if they know of any famous tunnels such as the Channel Tunnel. Do they know which animals make tunnels? What tunnels have they been through (for example, railway tunnels, motorway tunnels and so on)?

HOME LINKS
Explain to carers that the children have enjoyed playing with the tunnel, and ask them to bring in any large boxes that they may have in the future so that you can make another tunnel.

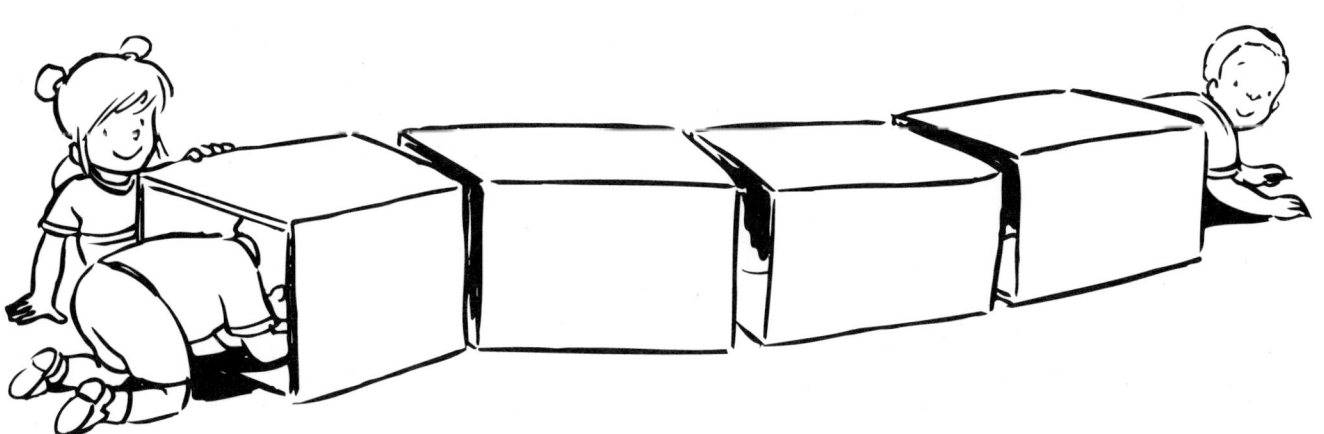

GROUP SIZE
Up to ten children.

TIMING
15 minutes.

WATCH OUT!

Learning objective
To travel around with increasing confidence.

What you need
A large, safe space outdoors; chalk.

What to do
Draw several boxes on the ground with the chalk and ask each child to stand in one of the boxes. Tell them that when you clap your hands you would like them to find a way of moving, without bumping into anyone else, to a different box. When you clap your hands again, the children should all have reached a different box. If they are not in a box when you clap you hands, they are out of the game. However, try not to let anybody be out on the first turn.

Explain to the children that they can travel in different ways, for example, backwards, forwards, sideways, hopping, skipping, jumping, marching, striding, twirling, dancing, on their toes, on their heels, on all fours and so on.

On the second turn, the children must move in a completely different way from the way that they moved before. Continue with the game until time runs out. For the last turn, clap your hands for the children to move and then clap them so quickly that everyone is out straight away!

Support
Ask the children to suggest lots of ways of moving, as a way of reminding children who might not have any ideas.

HOME LINKS
Demonstrate the game 'Grandmother's footsteps' to carers and ask them to play it at home with their children so that they can develop their skills of moving quietly and slowly and starting and stopping.

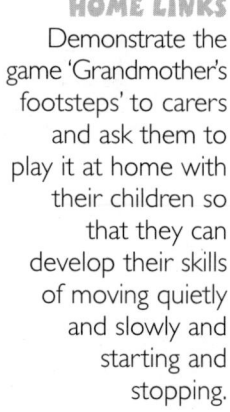

Extension
When the children have gained confidence in moving around the space, play 'Grandmother's footsteps'. The children should stand at one end of the space and you, as Grandmother, stand at the other. As soon as you turn your back on the children, they should begin to move towards you without making a sound, and attempt to touch you before you turn around. Every time you turn around, the children must freeze. If you catch anyone moving, they are out of the game. The first child to touch you becomes Grandmother.

GROUP SIZE
Up to four children.

TIMING
Ten minutes.

SANDWICH SPREAD

Learning objective
To handle tools and objects with increasing control.

What you need
Sliced bread; soft margarine or butter; fillings such as jam, lemon curd, cream cheese and banana; blunt knives; small paper plates; paper napkins; small name cards.

Preparation
Carry out this activity at a time when the children can have a lunch break or a tea party together. Check for any allergies or dietary requirements.

What to do
Ask the children if they know how to make a sandwich. Encourage them to verbalize the process, making sure that they get everything in the correct order. Let each child choose a filling for their sandwich from the selection, then invite them in turn to make their sandwich, with the rest of the children watching. First, encourage them to take two slices of bread, scrape some margarine or butter on the knife and spread it carefully on each of the slices. Then ask the child to take their chosen filling and put, or spread, some of it across one slice of bread. Make sure that they do not take too much and spoil it! If they have chosen banana as the filling, peel and slice the banana for them. Try to get the sandwich put together before the banana begins to discolour.

Next, put an opened paper napkin on one of the paper plates. Help the child to cut the sandwich into little squares or triangles, whichever they choose, then encourage them to put the pieces of sandwich neatly on to the paper napkin. Fold the napkin over the sandwich to keep it fresh until all the sandwiches are ready. Invite the child to choose their name card and place it in the centre of the wrapped-over napkin so that it will keep the napkin in place and ensure that they eat their own sandwich.

Support
Use hand-over-over support if the children find it difficult to spread and cut the bread, emphasizing how to hold the knife at an angle and spread carefully.

Extension
Help the children to stone and cut up some fruit to make a fruit salad with orange squash. Encourage them to serve the fruit salad themselves by spooning some of the fruit into small polystyrene dishes.

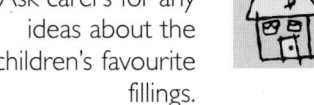

HOME LINKS
Ask carers for any ideas about the children's favourite fillings.

MULTICULTURAL LINKS
Use food from different cultures for the sandwich fillers, such as hummus or taramasalata.

SEW AND THREAD

Learning objective
To handle tools and objects with increasing control.

What you need
A small paper plate for each child; hole-punch; lengths of wool or ribbon in different colours and thicknesses; sticky tape.

Preparation
Punch approximately ten holes at random in the paper plates. Wind some sticky tape around one end of the lengths of wool so that it makes a firm ending that can be pushed through the holes.

What to do
Give each child a plate and a length of wool. Show the children how to thread the wool through the holes, using the taped end as a 'needle'. Pull the first piece of wool all the way through from the back and tape the end to the back of the plate. Invite the children to sew and thread the wool backwards and forwards through as many of the holes as they wish. Encourage them to begin using new colours at any time, threading the original piece through to the back and securing the end with sticky tape. Suggest that they pull different colours of wool through each hole and thread it into different patterns so that they complete a multicoloured piece of craft. If necessary, punch more holes into the plate, as required.

Support
Some of the children may find it difficult to thread the wool through from the back to the front – they will want to thread through to the back and then do the same thing again, ending up with the wool wound around the plate rather than threaded through. Be prepared to undo their mistakes and show them over and over again how to go from front to back and from back to front.

Extension
Once the children have developed the co-ordination required to do this activity, make some specific designs for them to sew and thread. Draw a chosen design on the front of the card and punch the holes so that the sewing and threading will give the child the shape that they want.

CHAPTER 6

Creative development

The activities in this chapter show how to develop the children's creative skills and give them the opportunity to contribute their own thoughts and opinons. Ideas include creating a 3-D model, making a group big picture and drawing patterns to music.

GROUP SIZE
Four children.

TIMING
Ten to 20 minutes.

HOME LINKS
Create an 'abstract art gallery' display and invite carers to visit the children's exhibition.

MULTICULTURAL LINKS
Use pictures from multicultural books to stimulate some pattern or representational ideas.

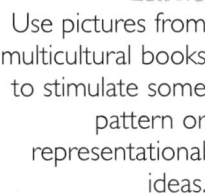

SLOSHY, SLOSHY

Learning objective
To explore colour in two dimensions.

What you need
Different-coloured pots of paint; thick paintbrushes; pots of water; art paper, sugar paper or newspaper; aprons.

Preparation
Make sure that the paints are mixed to a consistency that is not too thin.

What to do
Give each child a sheet of paper such as art paper, sugar paper or newspaper. Explain to the children that you would like them to paint whatever they want to and experiment with the colours of the paints. Discuss some ideas with them and suggest that the children who 'do not know what to paint' begin with any colour and brush it on to the paper to see what happens.

Point out the water pot to the children and show them how to rinse their brushes in the water when they decide to change colour. Encourage each child to do 'free' painting and make their design anything that they want it to be. Suggest that they experiment with mixing the colours if they feel the need to. Talk about what they think will happen if they mix one colour with another, or if they paint one colour over the top of another.

When the paintings are finished, discuss with the children the way that the colours have worked. Invite them to tell you what their paintings are about – are they pictures, patterns or representations? Which colours did they like using the most? Did any of them mix any colours and get new colours? What did they enjoy about the painting experience?

Support
Be aware of children who do not like the feel of the paint on their fingers and hands or who might be worried about 'getting dirty'. Help them to forget their inhibitions and to concentrate on producing something that they will like.

Extension
Different papers will produce different effects, so suggest that the children use textured wallpaper, or cut the paper into interesting shapes before they paint on it. Try varying the thickness of the paint, using more or less water, so that the children can experiment with different mixtures.

BUILD IT BIG

Learning objective
To explore shape in three dimensions.

What you need
Recyclable material such as boxes, tubes, polystyrene trays, polystyrene packing material, bubble wrap, egg-boxes, empty washing-up-liquid bottles, straws, buttons, scraps of fabric, buttons, scraps of shiny paper and cotton reels; scissors; strong glue; sticky tape; newspaper

Preparation
Make a base for the model with newspaper or card.

What to do
Encourage the children to look at the different materials that you have collected and discuss the shapes, sizes and textures. Tell them that, together, you are going to build a large model or sculpture using all the materials. Explain that it should not be flat, but it can be big, fat, wide, tall, short and so on. Invite the children to suggest ideas for what they could build and emphasize to them that the model does not have to be anything in particular – it can just be an interesting sculpture showing lots of shapes, colours, textures and so on.

Start building the model from the base up, and encourage the children to work on all sides of it, not just from the 'front'. Point out that it does not necessarily need to have a 'front' and a 'back' but can be made from whichever direction they choose. Help them to use proper 3-D shape words while creating the model, for example, 'cylinder', 'cube', 'cuboid' and so on.

When the model is finished, invite the children to decorate it with the scraps of fabric, paper and so on. Help them to decide on a name for their creation.

Support
The children may have difficulty deciding how to glue the cylinders or tubes to flat surfaces. Encourage them to see this as a problem-solving exercise and to think of solutions for themselves. If they still have difficulty, let them use sticky tape.

Extension
Invite the children to make a three-dimensional model out of two-dimensional materials. Can the children work out ways of folding card to make cubes, cylinders and other solid shapes, and then build a three-dimensional model with these?

GROUP SIZE
Four to six children.

TIMING
Ten to 15 minutes.

CUT AND STICK

Learning objective
To explore texture, shape and form in two dimensions.

What you need
Different-coloured, patterned and textured scraps of paper and fabric such as foil, shiny paper, transparent paper, wallpaper, bubble wrap, hessian, velvet, lace, embroidered fabric, knobbly wool, fur and net; glue sticks; glue pots; scissors; sugar paper.

Preparation
Cut the sugar paper into appropriate sizes for the children to stick their designs on. Cut the scraps into sizes that can be easily handled.

What to do
Tell the children that you would like them to make individual pictures or designs. These can be representations of things or places that they know, patterns, or a just a mixture of colours. Encourage them to use their imagination to make something that is of interest to them.

Give each child a piece of sugar paper. Invite them to choose scraps of paper and fabric and to cut them into different shapes and sizes of their choice. Then encourage them to stick the pieces on to the sugar paper in their own design. They may choose to stick them in a pattern, using colour or shape as their criteria, or to stick them randomly. As an alternative to using scissors, encourage the children to tear some of the scraps, to give a more ragged edge.

While the children are working, continue to use vocabulary such as 'big'. 'bigger', 'small', 'smaller', 'square', 'round', 'soft', 'smooth' and so on, so that they become familiar with and use the appropriate size, shape and texture words as they are creating.

Support
Help the children to cut their chosen fabric and paper into shapes.

Extension
Encourage the children to each work out their design beforehand, draw a brief idea of it and then see how their finished product matches or differs.

HOME LINKS
Ask carers for old magazines, scraps of coloured paper, wrapping paper, fabrics and so on for your collection. Suggest that they encourage their children to identify and name different shapes and textures at home.

MULTICULTURAL LINKS
Look for pictures of mosaics in different parts of the world to stimulate the children's imagination.

THREE-DIMENSIONAL DESIGN

Learning objective
To explore colour and shape in three dimensions.

What you need
Recycled and natural materials such as egg-boxes, straws, tubes, cereal boxes, sweet packets, leaves, twigs, cones and seed pods; card; felt-tipped pens or paints; strong glue.

Preparation
Cut a piece of card for each child to use as a base for their design.

What to do
Tell the children that you would like them to each make a three-dimensional picture or design on their own piece of card, which will serve as a base for it. Explain to them that they will have to choose shapes and colours carefully to make their designs as interesting as possible. Talk through the vocabulary of different shapes that they know and encourage them to identify as many colours as they can see among the materials.

Give the children the freedom to use as many shapes and colours as they wish. Invite them to choose their pieces of material by telling you the names of the colours and shapes. Help them to stick on the materials and remind them to build their designs outwards. Encourage them to fold bits of card and glue them just along the edges to attach on to the background to make the shapes 'stick out'.

While the children are handling the various bits of materials, emphasize vocabulary such as 'big', 'bigger', 'small', 'smaller', 'triangle', 'circle' and so on, and invite the children to explain and describe what they are doing.

HOME LINKS
Send the children's creations home and ask carers to encourage their children to describe to them the process of making these.

Support
Some children may find it difficult to choose and work independently. Give them lots of praise and encouragement to build up their self-confidence, and help them to understand that there is not a 'right' product: whatever they do *is* 'right'. If a child finds it difficult to get a starting-point, suggest that they choose a piece of material that they like, and help them to stick it on to their base. Encourage them to carry on looking for 'nice' pieces and sticking them on.

Extension
Help individual children to choose only one or two shapes and colours to ensure a completely different product at the end. Invite them to decorate the finished product with glitter, sequins, sticky stars and so on.

GROUP SIZE
Up to five children.

TIMING
20 to 30 minutes.

MAKE A BIG PICTURE

Learning objective
To explore colour and shape in two dimensions.

What you need
Scraps of different-sized, patterned and coloured paper; tissue paper; card; fabric; scissors; glue; large piece of card or sugar paper.

Preparation
Have the card or sugar paper ready as the background for the picture.

What to do
Explain to the children that you are going to make a big picture together that shows lots of colours and different shapes. Ask them if they would rather make a 'random' picture or a picture of something representational.

Discuss which shapes you could have in your picture – for example, circles, triangles, squares, oblongs, diamonds and so on – and help them to identify the colours that are in the materials.

Let the children suggest, in turn, desired shapes and colours, then cut them out. Show the children how to tear the paper carefully to achieve a ragged effect. Encourage them to glue their pieces of paper on to the card. Demonstrate how to create different effects by overlapping.

Give each child plenty of opportunity to contribute in choosing and sticking, and in verbalizing what they are doing. Continue cutting and sticking until the whole of the background card is covered.

Display the finished product where the children can easily see it and ask them to tell you what they think of it and talk about how they made it. Encourage them to verbalize the process that they have experienced.

Support
Be aware of the children whose fine motor skills or hand–eye co-ordination is not as developed as others'. Give them a little help and lots of praise.

Extension
Choose themes such as 'All reds', 'Round and round' and so on and make big pictures to create a display area.

HOME LINKS
Encourage the children to invite their carers to come to see their picture and to describe to them which parts they did. Remind them to use appropriate language to describe the colours and shapes.

MULTICULTURAL LINKS

Choose different festivals as themes for your picture and adapt your colours and shapes accordingly – for example, the picture of a Muslim wedding could be created in red and gold.

GROUP SIZE
Up to eight
children.

TIMING
Ten to 20 minutes.

STICK THE SHAPES

Learning objective
To use their imagination in art and design.

What you need
Sticky-backed paper shapes; sheet of paper or card for each child (for background).

Preparation
Cut the background paper into discs or triangles to make it more interesting if appropriate.

What to do
Give each child a sheet of background paper or card and several sticky shapes. Invite them to look at the shapes and to tell you what shapes and colours they can see.

Tell the children that they are each going to make a picture or design using their imagination on their background paper, simply by choosing shapes and colours and sticking them to the paper. Invite them to choose to do a 'random' design or something representational. Ask them for their ideas. Some children might want to do a picture of a toy, a clown, a star and so on; others might be happy to just choose and stick and see what their product becomes. Emphasize that all their ideas are equally acceptable. Draw simple outlines for the children who want them and explain to them how to fill them in.

Give the children as much freedom as possible, helping them to sort and match if they need you to and encouraging them to explain their ideas to you as they are creating.

Display the finished designs so that the group can easily see them and encourage the children to talk about and describe them. Why did they choose to do what they did? What do they like the most about their own design? What did they enjoy about doing it? Why?

Support
Some children may need help with hand–eye co-ordination, fine motor control or identifying colours. Be ready to support them where needed and give them lots of praise and encouragement.

Extension
Show the children how to make frames around their pictures or patterns by sticking shapes in a line all the way around the edges. If the children are able, encourage them to make a repeating pattern of colours or shapes, or both.

HOME LINKS
Put all the pictures into a folder to make an 'art book' and invite carers to come to your setting to look at their children's designs when they visit.

MULTICULTURAL LINKS
Look in reference books for pictures of traditional art from other cultures and share them with the children to stimulate their imagination.

GROUP SIZE
Up to 15 children.

TIMING
20 minutes.

I'M A FIREFIGHTER

Learning objective
To use imagination in role-play.

What you need
A variety of hats and headgear.

Preparation
If you do not have a large collection of hats and headgear, draw pictures on card or cut pictures from magazines and stick them on to card.

What to do
Invite the children to sit in a circle. Show them one of the hats and ask, 'Who would wear this kind of hat?'. Choose an obvious hat to begin with, such as a firefighter's helmet. Ask the children what kind of things the person who wears the hat would do, and what kind of movements they would make.

After exploring all the possibilities, invite the children to 'pretend' to put on the hat and become, as if by magic, that person. Talk through a series of the person's movements – for example, a firefighter would climb, drive, jump out of the appliance, lift, carry, push and pull. At the end of working through the movements, ask the children to freeze into the person's shape, act out taking off the hat, sit down and be themselves again.

Choose another hat which will give some contrasting movement ideas – for example, a contrast to a firefighter could be a king or a queen, wearing a crown, who would walk in a regal manner and perhaps wave to the crowds and shake people's hands. If appropriate, accompany the children's movements with a percussion instrument.

Support
Help the children to verbalize their ideas and encourage them to act out their imaginative ideas.

Extension
Make a series of headgear with the children, for example, a crown, party hat, chef's hat, jockey's cap, builder's hat, guard's hat, pirate's hat and so on, to use for role-play activities. Invite the children to suggest movements relating to these hats.

HOME LINKS
Ask carers if they have any headgear that they would be willing to let you borrow for discussion purposes, or any that they would be willing to donate for role-play activities.

MULTICULTURAL LINKS
Look for reference books that show different kinds of headgear that are worn in traditional situations, or for special occasions, and talk about them with the children.

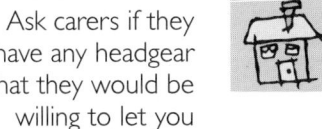

COLOURFUL MUSIC

Learning objective
To respond in a variety of ways to a piece of music.

What you need
A3 art paper or sugar paper; wax crayons; tape-recording of a piece of classical music that will bring a good response, for example, *Sorcerer's Apprentice* by Paul Dukas, *Four Seasons* by Vivaldi or *Carnival of the Animals* by Saint-Saëns; tape recorder.

Preparation
Ensure that the children have had practice at sitting still to listen to a piece of music and talk about it.

What to do
Give each child a piece of A3 paper and some wax crayons. Explain that you are going to play some music to them and you would like them to listen to it quietly and let their wax crayons move on their paper in any way that they want. Tell them that they can use the tips or the sides of the crayons. Explain that it is important to listen and let the crayons do whatever they want to do in time with the music.

Play the music and sit quietly yourself so that the children understand it is a very quiet time. Do the activity yourself, taking your mood from the music as you listen, so that the children recognize what they should do. Change your colours when appropriate and change the pressure or speed of your movements as the music changes. Some children will draw pictures and some will do abstract pieces, both are equally acceptable.

Invite some children to show and describe their pictures. Ask, 'What did the music make you feel like?', 'When it went fast, did your crayons go fast?', 'When it was slow did your crayons go slowly?', 'What did the music make you think about? Why?' and so on.

The important thing is to try to establish a link between listening and imagining so that the children make a reasonable response.

Support
If the children find it very difficult to sit still and listen, take them into a small group to sit very close to you so that if they are confused about the nature of the task, you can guide them very quietly without disturbing the others.

Extension
Play several different pieces music with the children to stimulate different kinds of crayoned responses.

LET'S MOVE

Learning objective
To recognize sound patterns and match movements to music.

What you need
A large, open space; tape-recording of a piece of music, for example, *Sorcerer's Apprentice* by Paul Dukas, *Four Seasons* by Vivaldi or *Carnival of the Animals* by Saint-Saëns; tape recorder.

What to do
Ask the children to get into a space. Make sure that they have enough room to be able to move and make shapes with their bodies without touching anyone else.

Tell the children that you would like them to listen to the music and move in whatever way it makes them want to go. Emphasize that they do not have to move the whole of their bodies if they do not want to, they can start with just moving their hands and arms.

Encourage the children to listen for heavy and light sounds that might mean stamping or tiptoeing, or fast and slow sounds that they could make jerky or flowing movements to. If they are moving in one direction, tell them to listen out for the music telling them, at any point, to turn, or to move in another direction. Does the music want them to make spiky or curvy shapes with their bodies? Are there spiky bits *and* curvy bits? While the children are doing their creative movements, emphasize the need to 'listen' and to move as the mood of the music makes them.

Support
Some of the children might feel quite insecure in listening and moving to music to begin with, so give them plenty of praise and encouragement and join into the spirit of the creative movement yourself to give them a role model. Let them sit on the floor and just move their hands and arms if they are too inhibited to move around.

Extension
Use simple percussion instruments to explore creative movements, for example, make beating sounds with woodblocks, drums and rhythm sticks; make melodic, ringing sounds with cymbals, finger cymbals, triangles and chime bars; make rattling, shaking sounds with tambourines, bells, maracas and castanets. Encourage the children to interpret the sounds and to create movements to them.

GROUP SIZE
Three or four
children at a time.

WHAT DOES IT SOUND LIKE?

Learning objective
To recognize repeated sounds and sound patterns.

TIMING
Ten minutes.

What you need
A tape-recording of a piece of music such as *Sorcerer's Apprentice* by Paul Dukas, *Four Seasons* by Vivaldi or *Carnival of the Animals* by Saint-Saëns; tape recorder.

What to do
Invite the children to identify different kinds of sounds in the music, deciding whether it is speeding up or slowing down, whether it is 'high' or 'low', whether it is 'happy' or 'sad', whether it sounds like any particular thing (such as an animal in *Carnival of the Animals*) and so on. Listen with the children to a piece of music. Ask them, 'What does this music make you think about?', 'Why does it make you think about that?' and 'What does it remind you of?'. When you have explored those ideas, ask, 'How does this music make you feel?' and 'Why do you think it makes you feel like that?'. Also ask, 'Do you like this music?', 'What do you like or dislike about it?', 'Do you like all of it or certain parts?', 'Which parts?' and so on. Remember that there is no 'right' response. Encourage the children to respond in their own ways. This will depend upon the extent of their experiences and their imagination.

Can the children suggest what kinds of instruments might be making the sounds? Ask, 'Is there just one instrument in some places, or all of the orchestra?', 'How do you think that the musicians all keep together?', and 'Can you hear when the music is "flowing", "quivering", or making "staccato" or "swirling" sounds?'. Can they identify when the music is going faster and more slowly? Can they identify when it gets louder and quieter? Encourage the children to verbalize their ideas about what the music is doing and what feelings it is stimulating.

Support
The children may find this quite difficult to begin with, so help them with any vocabulary that they are searching for and encourage them to discuss the music within a small group.

Extension
Ask the children to each draw and colour a picture, or dictate a story to you, that will tell someone else about the piece of music. Create a book with the pictures or stories, give it the title of the piece of music, and name the children as authors.

HOME LINKS
Invite carers to come and listen to the piece of music with a small group of children and look at the book at the same time.

MULTICULTURAL LINKS
Play music from different traditions and cultures to the children at quiet times, encouraging thoughtful responses.

What should we do?

Beetle game

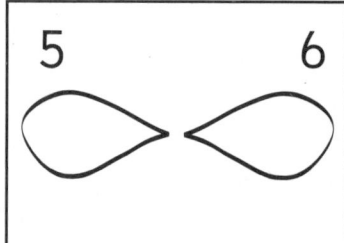

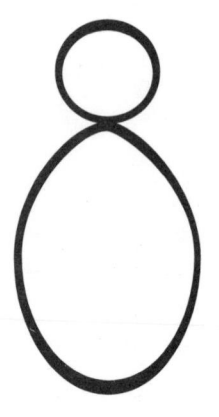

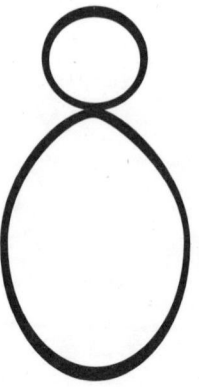

This is how I feel

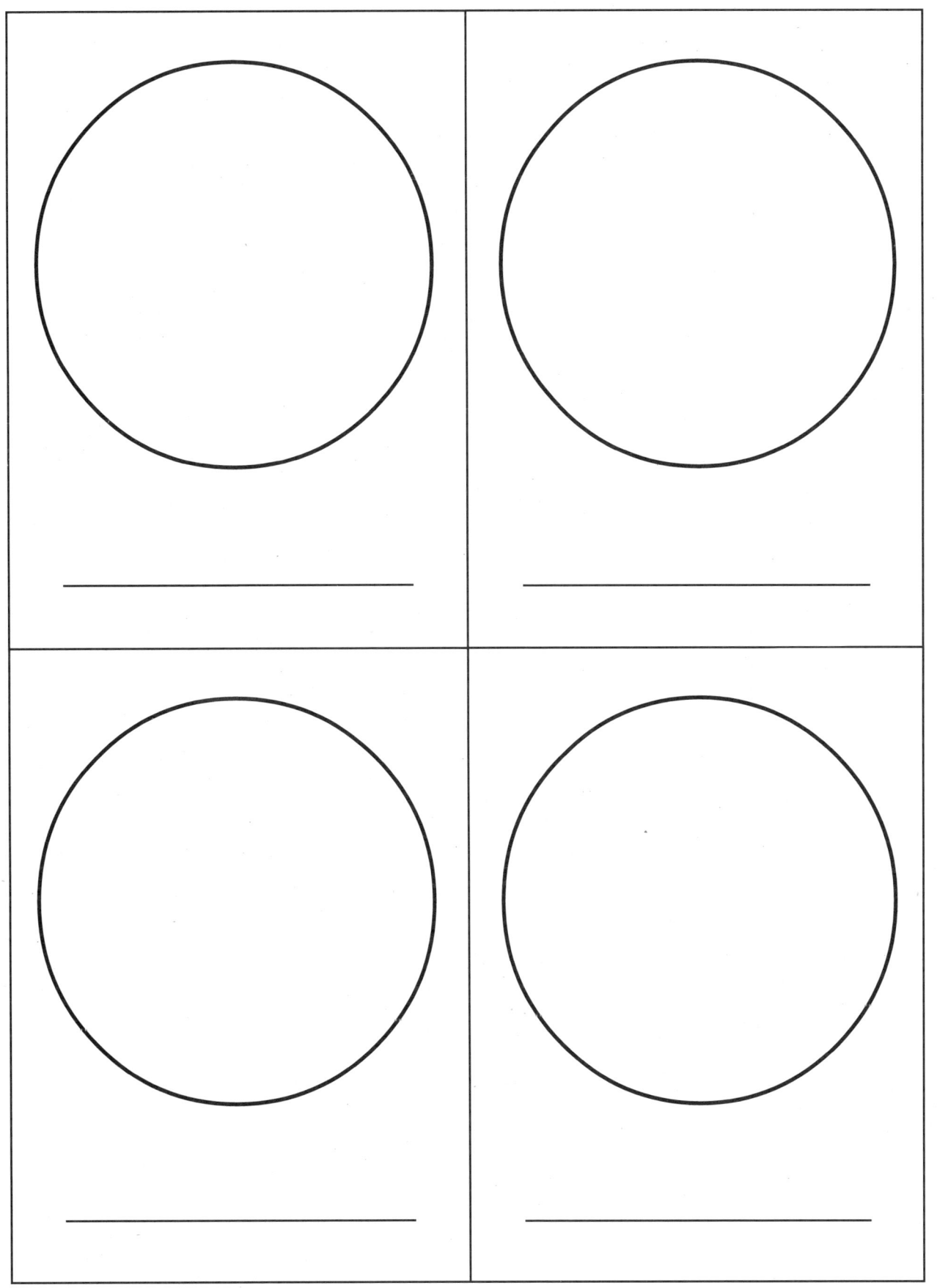

Match the boxes (1)

1	2	3
4	5	6
7	8	9

Match the boxes (1)

Match the boxes (2)

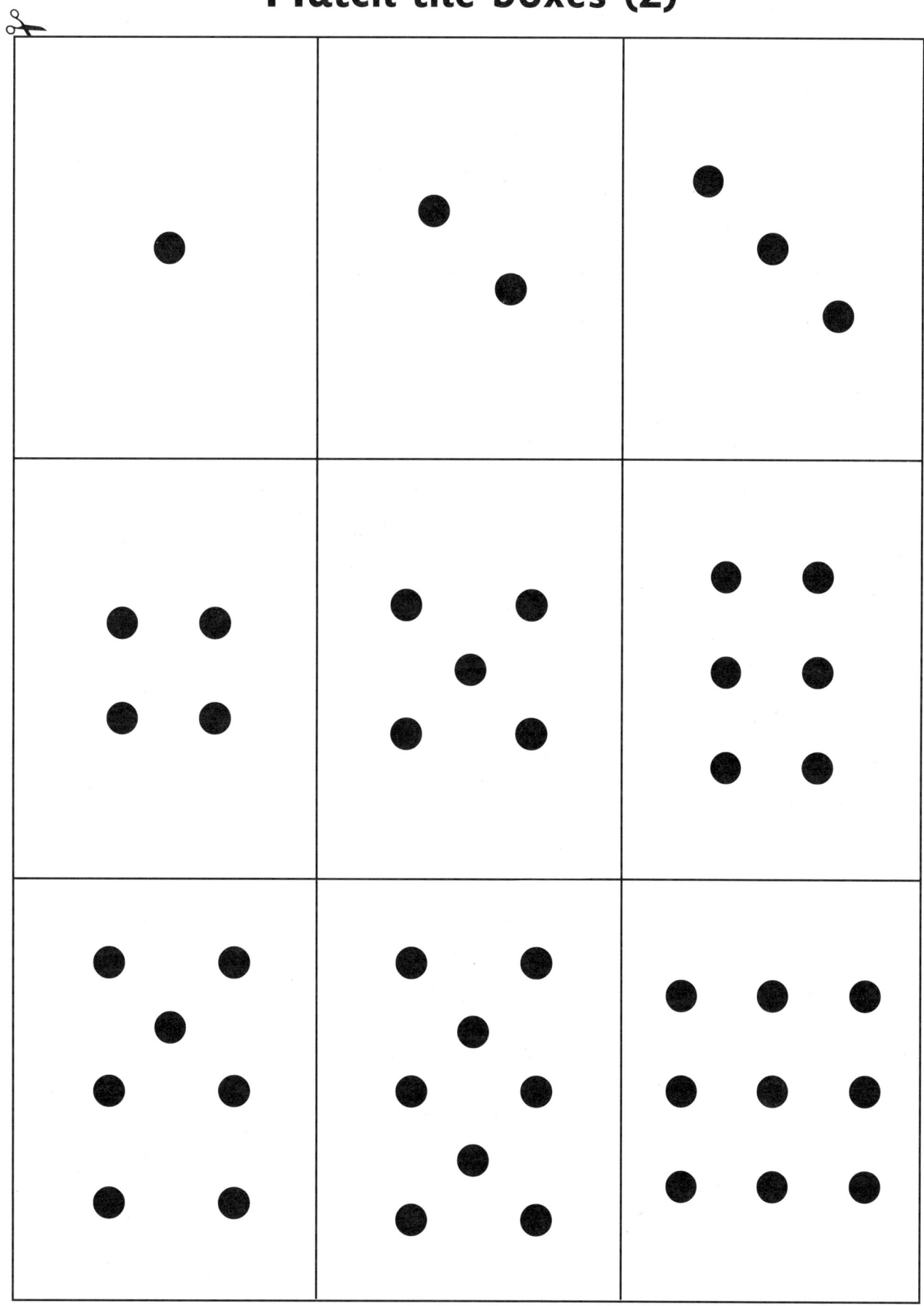

Match the boxes (2)

How many T-shirts?

How heavy is your dinosaur?

How heavy is your dinosaur?

My plant and animal

This is a picture of my plant	My plant is
	_____
	_____
	_____
	_____
This is a picture of my animal	My animal is
	_____
	_____
	_____
	_____

My plant and animal

Look alike

Draw a circle around the one which is the same.

Animal features

Spot the difference

Look at each picture and circle the one that is different.

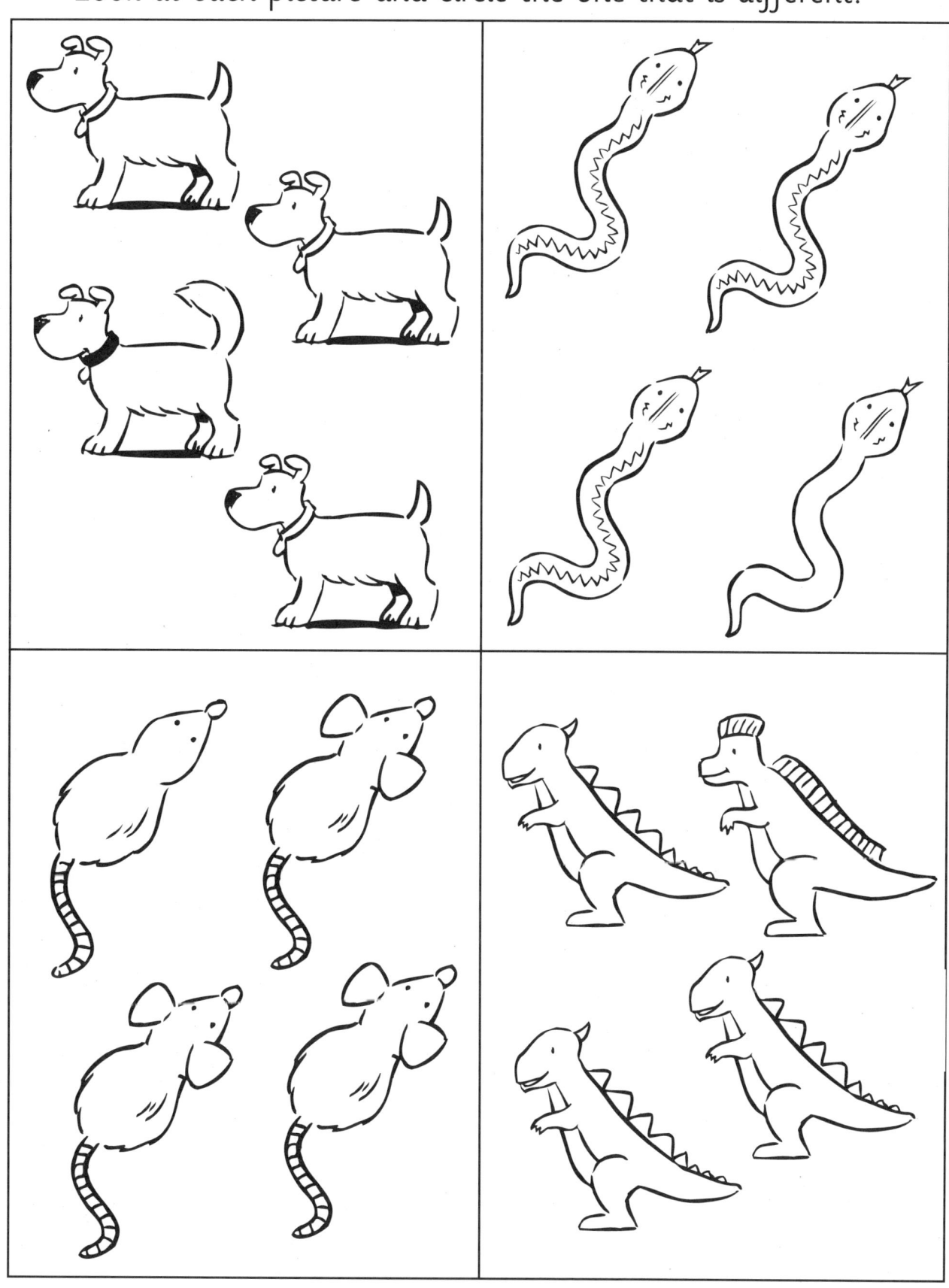

 # At the bottom of the garden

Outside, I found

a _____	a _____
a _____	a _____

I also saw a

My favourite is the _____ because

_____